ↄ✧ↄ

"I believe that every church would benefit by integrating the concepts of *Conversational Evangelism* into its existing evangelistic programs and strategies!"

JOSH MCDOWELL
Josh McDowell Ministry

"*Conversational Evangelism* is a winsome and effective presentation of how skeptics perceive the Gospel and how we might help them discover its truth for themselves. While recognizing the vital role of the Holy Spirit in the process, the Geislers illustrate how asking probing questions and pointing out the inconsistencies between belief and behavior till the ground and help remove long-entrenched barriers to the Gospel. I enthusiastically recommend their pre-evangelism methodology."

RAVI ZACHARIAS
Ravi Zacharias International Ministries

"*Conversational Evangelism* hits the mark! Similar to leading seeker small groups, this approach—asking relevant questions so seekers can discover biblical truths for themselves—is one of the most effective and powerful ways to reach out and help seekers cross the line of faith."

GARRY POOLE
Evangelism Director at Willow Creek Community Church
and author of *Seeker Small Groups*

"*Conversational Evangelism* is refreshing in its format and content. I have not found anything that comes close to dealing with the legitimate barriers that most people have *before* they can give the Gospel a hearing."

ERIN KERR
Evangelism Pastor, Saddleback Church

"*Conversational Evangelism* is a fantastic way for bringing apologetics to our non-believing friends, colleagues, and neighbors. With very little work, those with a basic knowledge of apologetic topics can now enjoy applying that knowledge more than ever. I know of no other program quite like it."

MIKE LICONA
Apologetics & Interfaith Evangelism, Director
North American Mission Board (SBC)

"Truth is best communicated in the realm of interpersonal relationships. And the best conduit for establishing relationships is the fine art of soul-searching conversation. As such, *Conversational Evangelism* is a vital tool for communicating the Gospel in a nonthreatening, pre-evangelistic manner. This fresh pre-evangelism model is seeker-sensitive, Word-centered, and purpose-driven. It is designed to win a hearing, much as Jesus did when He engaged in conversational evangelism with the Samaritan woman at Jacob's well (John 4)."

REV. EDMUND CHAN
Senior Pastor, Covenant Evangelical Free Church, Singapore
and author of *Built to Last* and *Growing Deep in God*

"Most courses on evangelism teach us how to harvest, which creates a mentality that is very event and closure driven. Yet in real life, conversion is much more a process that takes place over time. *Conversational Evangelism* opens our eyes to the amount of work we have to invest in understanding a person prior to the time that we can really present the Gospel. We look forward to turning it into a core course we will encourage all our members to attend."

PETER LIN
Congregational Pastor, Grace Baptist Church, Singapore

"One of the burdens of pastors is how to motivate their congregation to share their faith. Norman and David Geisler have come up with an approach that I strongly commend to help train and spur our people to win the lost amongst us."

DAN FOO
Senior Pastor, Bethesda (Bedok-Tampines) Church, Singapore

"This is the first time I have seen apologetics being used as a significant tool for personal evangelism. It has altogether reshaped my understanding of apologetics and evangelism. I wholeheartedly recommend this training to any Christian or church committed to soul-winning."

REV. NG KOON SHENG
Anglican Minister, Saint Andrews Cathedral, Singapore

☙

Conversational
EVANGELISM

NORMAN GEISLER
DAVID GEISLER

HARVEST HOUSE PUBLISHERS
EUGENE, OREGON

CONVERSATIONAL EVANGELISM
Copyright © 2009 by Norman Geisler and David Geisler
Published by Harvest House Publishers
Eugene, Oregon 97402
www.harvesthousepublishers.com

Library of Congress Cataloging-in-Publication Data
Geisler, Norman L.
Conversational evangelism / Norman and David Geisler.
   p. cm.
ISBN 978-0-7369-2399-6 (pbk.)
1. Evangelistic work. I. Geisler, David. II. Title.
BV3790.G43 2009
269.'2—dc22
                                                    2008020668

Printed in the United States of America

11 12 13 14 15 16 17 / BP-NI / 10 9 8 7 6 5 4 3

I dedicate this book to my wife, Charlene, for her love, support, and sacrifice apart from which this book would not have been possible.—David Geisler

℘

I dedicate this with great appreciation to my faithful wife, Barbara, who has been proofreading my manuscripts for forty years.—Norman Geisler

Acknowledgments

We would like to thank the following people for their combined insights and feedback that made this book possible:

David Ostroot for the tireless hours he put into editing an early draft of this material

Eric Patterson for his informative suggestions

David Mendez for his helpful input

Dave Montoya for his valuable insights and model

Greg Meece, Steve Morrison, Gina Jones, Kent Vanderwaal, and James Coffman whose valuable contributions led to the development of our Conversational Evangelism model

Glenn McGorty for his inspiration and example

Rod Morris of Harvest House for his excellent editing

Barbara Geisler for careful proofreading of the manuscript

Contents

Foreword
by Ravi Zachariast

The first few times I got behind a pulpit to preach, I was preparing for a career in business. However, each time I finished delivering the message, a handful of people would tell me that the gift of evangelism upon me was very evident. The more I preached, the more I heard the same comment. Although it was encouraging to hear, I really did not understand the implications of what they were saying. Preaching was so new to me that I had not gone deep enough to reflect on the affirmation they were giving me. I was still just a young lad from India who had been transformed by my new life in Christ, planning to work in a field for which I had studied. So out of courtesy I would just nod a sincere thank you and leave it at that.

Yet, in truth, a special sense of mission and conviction would rise up in me each time I stood to proclaim the beautiful Gospel of Jesus Christ. I had an intense urge to persuade. From the very beginning, I knew I wanted to speak to people who were on a quest, people whose minds were gripped by the hard questions of life, people who were hurting inside and needed someone who could speak to those issues. God was shaping that call in me by using other people to help me understand what it meant to do the work of an evangelist.

The word *evangelism* often stirs strong and conflicting emotions, even for the follower of Christ. Engaging with others in this seemingly daunting task may incite enthusiasm as well as discomfort. Yet one thing is certain, as article four of the Lausanne Covenant recognizes: "Our Christian presence in the world is indispensable to evangelism, and so is that kind of dialogue whose purpose is to listen sensitively in order to understand. But evangelism itself is the proclamation of the historical, biblical Christ as Saviour and Lord, with a view to persuading people to come to him personally and so be reconciled to God."

As such, evangelism done properly will awaken a sense of need within the hearer, and more importantly, evangelism done persuasively will show that if Christianity is true, it will provide an answer to that need. Christ must be seen not only to be the answer; His words must also be seen to be true. This is a definitive difference because the claim of the believer—of a "new birth"—is unique. After all, no Buddhist or Hindu or Muslim claims his or her life of devotion to be supernatural, though they may often live a more consistent life than believers in Christ.

As followers of Jesus Christ, not only do we claim the truth of a super-natural transformation, we must remind ourselves that defending the faith we believe also calls upon us to live the faith we defend. First Peter 3:15 gives us the charge: "But in your hearts set apart Christ as Lord. Always be prepared to give an answer (*apologia*) to everyone who asks you to give the reason for the hope that you have. But do this with gentleness and respect." Notice that before one is qualified to give an answer, there is a prerequisite. The lordship of Christ over the life of His follower is foundational to all answers given.

Once we hold that word and deed in balance, the opportunities are immense all around us to speak to the honest questioner and even the evasive one. The starting point for the follower of Christ is that belief and conduct must be consistent. From there, the all-important key in evangelism is to listen beyond the question to the questioner. To answer the question but not the questioner is as much of a breakdown as a faith that is not lived out in the practical.

One of the most extensive conversations Jesus had—His conversation with the Samaritan woman at the well—greatly surprised His own disciples (see John 4:1-26). You recall that the woman raised one question after another, as if they were really her problem. It would have been easy for the Lord to call her bluff with some castigating words. Instead, like a sensitive and nimble-handed goldsmith, He rubbed away the markings of sin and pain in her life until she was amazed at how much true gold He brought out in her. He gave her hope, knowing all along who she really was on the inside. The value of the person was an essential part of Jesus' message—and this must be so for us as well. Then we will be able to listen sensitively in order to understand what is really being asked, and reach those we are listening to so that they might listen as well.

We often underestimate the role we may play in clearing the obstacles in someone's spiritual journey. A seed sown here, a light shone there may be all that is needed to move that person one step further along the way. Often the conversation will move from the smokescreens of supposed questions of the mind to the real questions of the heart. Effective evangelism finds the bridge to connect both. The best apologetic is able to travel the journey with the questioner, connecting the head with the heart.

When one considers those who have made an impact in the field of evangelism and apologetics, the names of Francis Schaeffer, C.S. Lewis, and Norman Geisler come readily to mind. Norman Geisler has had a significant impact and share in my life. I studied under him as my professor, and he is, in my estimation, one of the finest apologists ever. I look back with deep gratitude to God for the role Dr. Geisler has played and continues to play in my life. His discipline is exemplary, his expertise wide. Anyone who hears him is amazed at the range of Scripture he draws upon and the breadth of philosophy within his grasp. Of great value to any reader of his books is to see how his philosophical prowess never overrides his deep commitment to the Scriptures. It was the balance between his love of the Scriptures and his rigorous argumentation of God's Word that gave me the imperatives I needed to preach and teach, especially in areas of great resistance. My life as an evangelist and apologist has benefited greatly from his influence and from observing and studying his writings.

In this work, I am especially thrilled that his son, David, has followed in his father's footsteps, also blazing new paths with his work through Meekness and Truth Ministries. My colleagues and I have had the privilege of working alongside David in Singapore and India and have found his material invaluable in various settings. Our students who have studied under David have nothing but the deepest admiration for the way he understands the listener and gives answers that bring the truth to the level of the questioner's felt need.

Each generation needs voices like theirs that never forget the past but speak to the present in preparation for the future. I am so pleased to write the foreword to *Conversational Evangelism*. It is truly a winsome and effective presentation of how skeptics perceive the Gospel and how we believers might help them discover its life-transforming truth for themselves. While recognizing the vital and indispensable role of the Holy Spirit in the process, the Geislers illustrate that asking probing questions and pointing out the inconsistencies between belief and behavior tills the ground and helps remove long-entrenched barriers to the Gospel. I enthusiastically recommend their pre-evangelism understanding and study. Anyone who wants to do evangelism in this age of graduate-level skepticism without losing the simplicity and sublimity of the Gospel will find this book a treasure.

Ravi Zacharias, author and speaker

Introduction

I now understand better what is holding back many people from coming to Christ, i.e., the barriers they encounter in understanding and then in embracing the Christian faith. As I become more equipped and emboldened to add the spiritual dimension in my conversation with friends and colleagues, I discover that people are willing to engage in conversations of a spiritual nature much more often than I previously thought.

—ELDER HIAN-CHYE

In spite of your great trepidation, your friend tells you it will be an experience worth remembering. You ignore your fear and tell yourself you'll be okay. So you step into the roller coaster and strap yourself down knowing that if you just make it through to the end in one piece, that will be a great success. You may not even entertain the possibility that you will enjoy the ride. The bottom line is to just get through it so you can say that you've done it.

In many ways doing evangelism these days can be much like riding a roller coaster. You don't really want to do it, and you certainly don't expect to enjoy it. Worst of all, through the ups and downs, you always feel like you end up where you originally began.

But what if evangelism could be different? What if it could be something you actually enjoy doing? What if it could be something you do, not only because you have an obligation to do it, but more importantly because you see in very tangible ways how your obedience to Christ can make a difference in the lives of those you care most to reach? What if it can be something you enjoy doing so much that you end up doing it every day for the rest of your life? What if, as a result of learning how to effectively build bridges to the Gospel, you feel more and more compelled to make the most of every encounter with your nonbelieving friends to help them take steps to the cross?

This book is an attempt to make this a possibility in the life of the average Christian who increasingly finds it difficult to witness to those in a post-Christian world. Provided that we have the right framework for what evangelism is and have been equipped to engage people in our contra-Christian culture, we believe that not only can we make progress in our witness to people, but we can even enjoy the ride.

Furthermore, we are also convinced that we can be good witnesses even when we don't always desire to be. Even when we're not looking for open doors, we can still have an impact on people we regularly rub shoulders with if we remember at least two things. First, we must remember to expand our definition of success in witnessing (we'll talk more about this in chapter 1). Second, we must remember not to cover up any light that has already been revealed to our non-Christian friends and remain willing to make the most of all the divine opportunities God gives us (1 Peter 3:15).

In order to maximize your efforts in using this book, we want to clarify a few things. First, while some of the concepts in the following chapters may seem difficult to understand, or even mechanical and imper-sonal, *carefully learn each step in order* (don't skip ahead) and practice all the exercises at the end of each chapter under the Reflection and Applica-tion sections. Also, when applicable, refer to the resources in the back of the book that may go with a particular chapter. Working through these will help you get a better handle on the concepts in each chapter before you venture into the next chapter and learn other new concepts.

Second, developing a new skill takes practice, so don't short-circuit the process. Take the time to learn this material well enough that it becomes a part of the fabric of your witnessing style. Remember that the art of engaging others in spiritual dialogue takes time and practice. This is not a skill we can master overnight. So don't be discouraged or frustrated if your first attempt to apply these principles doesn't turn out exactly the way you thought it would. Don't be surprised if people don't respond to your approach in a more positive manner than you originally thought. We must learn to crawl before we can walk, and we have to learn how to walk before we can run with confidence. So don't rush the learning process or get disheartened that you're not advancing more quickly in learning to use this approach.

Also, keep in mind that *our struggles in evangelism are not primarily about methodology but about maturity.* Do we have a heart for God and do we care about the things God cares about (lost people)? If we have God's heart, we will do whatever we can to advance His kingdom purposes in every conversation we have with our nonbelieving friends.

Once we have the right posture in serving our Master and Savior and a passion for the lost around us, we may find the methods described in this book helpful for better engaging others in spiritual conversation. But please don't confuse what our priorities should be. First, we should ask God to develop in us a greater heart and passion for the lost. Once this happens, we will find it easier to apply the principles in this book. Once our heart is right with God, we can begin to talk to people in a more effective way so that many may believe (Acts 14:1).

Are you ready to take that next step of faith? The journey begins today!

Chapter 1

The Need for Pre-Evangelism in a Postmodern World

The Need to Overhaul Our Evangelism Paradigms

Something is missing today in our approach to evangelism. Methods and tools used in the '60s and '70s don't have the impact they once did. Our models for evangelism need an overhaul. While proclaiming the Gospel may be relatively simple, getting to that proclamation is not. As a result, it's imperative that we modify our existing models to include other elements necessary for success. Such a paradigm shift is needed for at least three reasons.

Many People Are Less Interested in a Simple Presentation of the Gospel

First, there is less and less interest in the Gospel message itself. Consequently, Christians today find their traditional approaches to evangelism somewhat limiting. It was common 30 to 40 years ago to use a simple tract to share the Gospel with others, especially on college campuses. Many baby boomers were won to Christ back in their youth because someone shared the Gospel with them in this way. Today it is much more difficult to reach people by just sharing a simple four-point Gospel presentation. This is true of people in the East or West.

A director for a large Christian ministry on a campus in the U.S. once confessed, "Only on a good day do I help someone take a step closer to Christ." Expectations have changed, even among college workers in the last 30 years. And a former seminary student in Singapore suggests that something is missing in our approach to reaching students in the East: "As a campus ministry staff person, I am trained in using a simple Gospel presentation and some apologetic skills, but I have problems trying to integrate them during evangelism. When people indicate that they are not interested, I can only ask them for the reason and then invite them for an evangelistic Bible study or share my personal testimony." She felt limited in her ability to reach students with the training she had received in evangelism, especially with those who were not yet ready to hear about Christ.

We are not advocating that we get rid of all the evangelistic tools we've used in the past. God can and does use these tools with those who have some receptivity to the Gospel. What is needed today, however, is a tool that can supplement what we already know about evangelism, especially when presenting the Gospel to those who are indifferent, skeptical, or even hostile to the claims of Christ. Not everyone is at the same point in their openness to the Gospel, and we need to use different approaches depending on someone's spiritual openness.

The World We Live in Has Changed

The second reason we need to develop a new model of evangelism is that the world we live in has changed in ways that often create barriers to the Gospel. The world today can be characterized by a rejection of moral absolutes, a deep religious skepticism, and an indifference or outright rejection of objective truth.

The Rejection of Moral Absolutes. Sheryl Crow's song, "Every Day Is a Winding Road," sums up the situation well in these words: "These are the days that anything goes."[1] We live in a different world than our parents did, a different world with a different and relativistic value system. Unfortunately, our young people have discarded many of the moral values that make up the fabric of our society. This rejection of moral beliefs has caused some major repercussions to our effectiveness in evangelism.

Cultural anthropologist Gene Veith says, "It is hard to proclaim the forgiveness of sins to people who believe that, since morality is relative, they have no sins to forgive...It is not the lunatic fringe rejecting the very concept of (absolute) truth, but two-thirds of the American people." [2] Another has said, "As we approach the twenty-first century, it does not take a rocket scientist to recognize that our entire culture is in trouble. We are staring down the barrel of a loaded gun, and we can no longer afford to act like it's loaded with blanks."[3]

One of the characters in Fyodor Dostoyevsky's novel *The Brothers Karamazov* contends that if there is no God, everything is permitted. Unfortunately, this pervasive perspective has led to many serious consequences. Newspapers remind us daily of the painful repercussions of a culture teetering toward moral bankruptcy.

It is especially difficult to share Christ with those who have been brought up in an atmosphere of relativism. An increasing number of non-Christians regard our message as irrelevant, judgmental, or no better than any other perspective. As a result, many in our culture are not predisposed to give the message of Christ a hearing. This makes our task in evangelism more difficult than ever. Those who have been inoculated against the very concept of ultimate truth may be indifferent to the "Good News" if they do not realize there is such a thing as "bad news." Consequently, we must defend the concept of absolute truth as we try to explain more clearly to those we witness to why we believe that Christianity is true and other religions are false.

Skepticism Toward Truth. We also live in a world that is becoming increasingly more skeptical about objective truth, especially religious truth. This skepticism is especially prevalent in the academic community. We must follow the lead of the "men of Issachar, who understood the times and knew what Israel should do" (1 Chronicles 12:32). Part of understanding the times we live in is to realize that people generally do not take at face value what we say is true, especially if it is religious truth. It is common to believe that something cannot be known to be true unless it can be verified through the scientific method of repeated observations. Furthermore, a great number claim that we can't come to any conclusion about any religious truth.

This skeptical disposition has led many to question whether we can really know that what was said about Jesus actually happened 2000 years ago. After I gave a student some evidence for Christ's resurrection, he said, "If I were living at the time of Christ, I could make decisions about who Jesus is, but it's been 2000 years. So, we cannot really make decisions like that anymore."

With the recent onslaught of books, movies, and documentaries such as *The Da Vinci Code, The Gospel of Judas,* and *The Lost Tomb of Jesus,* skepticism about the history of the Christian faith is at an all-time high. In general, people in the first century did not have the obstacles that we have 2000 years later to believe what the New Testament writers recorded about the life of Christ. Even some non-Christian writers at that time acknowledged that Jesus was a wonder worker.[4]

The apostles and disciples also did not have to prove the existence of God or the possibility of miracles to their Jewish and god-fearing Greek audiences; many of them already believed in a theistic God. They also believed that something miraculous happened as evidenced by the empty tomb. This was common knowledge of the time.

Nonbelievers nowadays struggle with the question, "Can we know truth at all, even if it does exist?" Some people today deny that we can know historical truths of recent times, such as the Holocaust, even though there are still people alive who survived Nazi prison camps.[5] This over-arching skepticism in our society has made our task of evangelism more difficult in this new millennium.

An Indifference Toward Truth. Our society has not only rejected truth and moral absolutes and developed a deep skepticism, especially regarding religious matters, but it has also developed indifference toward truth in general. The main problem in evangelism today is the "ever-increasing number of people who are simply not interested in hearing about Jesus because they are quite happy with their own views."[6] As a result, some will say, "It's nice for you that you believe in truth," or "It's nice that it works for you, but it doesn't work for me or mean anything to me. It may certainly be true for you, but not for me."[7]

One international student said, "I agree with the point that religion is good to the society…but what that religion is is not that important. It's better to have people believe in something, rather than nothing. After I came to the U.S., I found that people who believe in God are generally better off than those who believe in nothing. But it has nothing to do with the existence of God. It's a kind of social psychology."

These events should be no surprise to those who believe the words of Paul in 2 Timothy 4:3-4, "For the time will come when men will not put up with sound doctrine. Instead, to suit their own desires, they will gather around them a great number of teachers to say what their itching ears want to hear. They will turn their ears away from the truth and turn aside to myths." This was true in the first century, but it is even more true today. As the moral fabric of our society deteriorates, we will need to do more to supplement our evangelism just to get a hearing.

These are global changes. The sad truth is that the tsunami of postmodernism is blowing from the West to the East with devastating impact. Christian apologist Ravi Zacharias says, "You are living in a time when the West is looking more like the East, and the East is quietly imitating the West."[8]

A former seminary student in the East, who is a college worker at a church in Singapore, sent the following urgent e-mail one day about her difficulties in witnessing to college students.

> Many students [in Singapore] don't think that there is a standard of right and wrong. Rather, they believe that this is up to the individual. This means they do hold a standard of right and wrong themselves, but they feel that each person's standard of right and wrong differs from the other. Personally, I feel stuck as to how to proceed on with the conversation. It's like saying that this food is nice for me but may not be nice for you. They relegate the standard of right and wrong to personal preference. *I find that I'm*

shaken. Not in terms of my faith, but in terms of how to answer such questions.

It is clear that our approach needs an overhaul. Is the church ready to respond to these postmodern influences, especially in the way it goes about doing evangelism today?

An Increasing Intolerance Toward Those Who Believe in Absolute Truth

Third, the world's perspective on those who believe in an absolute truth has also made our task more daunting. Not only do we live in a world characterized by a rejection of moral absolutes, deep skepticism, and an indifference to or rejection of truth, there is also intolerance toward those who claim to know the truth. For us as Christians to claim that Jesus is the only way to God sounds arrogant and intolerant to our non-Christian postmodern friends.[9] We are considered arrogant to even profess to know the truth. Worse, it proves that we claim to be better than others or at the very least that we are intolerant of other beliefs.

If you add up all these factors, it is clear that the evangelistic task today is more difficult than ever before. Our approach to evangelism in the new millennium needs to be reworked. What is needed to more clearly communicate the Gospel to this postmodern generation is an emphasis on *pre-evangelism,* or training in what we call here *conversational evangelism.*[10]

Defining Pre-evangelism

What is pre-evangelism? If evangelism is planting seeds of the Gospel, then pre-evangelism is *tilling the soil of people's minds and hearts to help them be more willing to listen to the truth* (1 Corinthians 3:6). Because of the kind of world we live in today, we may not be able to plant the seeds of the Gospel until we work the soil of people's minds and hearts. Failure to prepare the soil may lead to closed doors for planting seeds today and a reluctance to consider the Gospel message in the future.

Once we understand the times in which we live, we will make pre-evangelism an essential part of the evangelism training in our churches, seminaries, and mission organizations to more effectively reach people for Christ in the new millennium.[11]

Redefining What We Mean by Evangelism

For pre-evangelism to be fruitful, at least two things need to be done. First, we need to redefine what we mean by *evangelism*. Most of us have been taught that evangelism is "proclaiming the good news and inviting others to trust Christ." Yet, a valuable element is missing in that definition. The missing element is simply that *evangelism is a process.* The apostle Paul said, "I planted the seed, Apollos watered it, but God made it grow" (1 Corinthians 3:6). You and I may not be able in one conversation to share all of the Gospel with our nonbelieving friends and then invite them to trust Christ. But we may be able to help them take a step closer with each encounter.

If we equate evangelism with reaping, we may get discouraged in our witness when those we speak with are not interested at first. We may feel like a failure because we are not "doing evangelism." As a result, many of us may pull back from the task of evangelism, partly because we don't like to fail.

Christian writer and Campus Crusade for Christ staff member Tim Downs concurs with this misperception about evangelism. He says, "We have come to believe that there are only two kinds of Christians: the harvesters and the disobedient. We must begin to teach, with great urgency, that every laborer should learn to reap and that God will call some to exercise this role exclusively—but everyone can learn to sow right now, right where they are."[12]

In the world we live in today, we may have to plant many spiritual seeds for a period of time before someone will seriously consider the person of Christ. We may have to till the ground before we have the opportunity to plant a seed. We are not called to bring all persons to Christ but simply to bring Christ to all persons.

In light of these concerns, it would be better to redefine evangelism in the following way: *Evangelism is every day and in every way helping your nonbelieving friends to take one step closer to Jesus Christ.*[13] It may take some time for your nonbelieving friends to seriously consider the claims of Christ and make the decision to invite Him into their lives (John 1:12) and allow Him to change them from the inside out (Philippians 2:13). This means in practice that every day we need to ask ourselves, "What do I need to do today to help my nonbelieving friends take one step closer to Jesus?"

Changing Our Strategy in Evangelistic Encounters

Our goal in our evangelistic encounters need not be to get the whole Gospel message out at one time (and possibly alienate those we're trying to reach). At times the Holy Spirit will prompt us to go further, but we need discernment to know how much a person can hear from us at one time without becoming defensive and pulling back from the conversation. Rather, *we should take the long-term view and leave that person with the desire to continue the conversation.*

This is a different way of thinking about evangelism, but one that we believe all Christians must learn in order to more effectively reach this postmodern generation. This means that when we engage people in spiritual discussions at work or at school or in our neighborhood, we conduct our conversation in such a way that they desire to continue the spiritual dialogue the next time we see them. Too many times we have been taught methods of communicating the Gospel that are offensive. As a result it is not uncommon to find nonbelievers who do not want to have anything to do with Christians or the Christian message because of their distasteful first exposure to the Good News.

This does not mean, however, that we will never run into people who are hostile when we try to talk with them about Christ using a pre-evangelistic approach. In Acts 17 there were at least three different responses to the apostle Paul's message even though he took the time to build pre-evangelistic bridges to the Gospel. So we too should expect an occasional angry reaction from others when we speak the truth of Jesus (John 15:18-21). But we should do all we can to make our manner of communicating the Gospel as inoffensive as possible even if the message of our Gospel may be offensive to some (1 Corinthians 1:23-24; 1 Peter 2:8).

Changing our style of evangelism doesn't preclude the Holy Spirit from prompting us to say something to our friends that may be difficult for them to hear (and maybe for us to say). The blood of the Christian martyrs through the centuries is testimony to the fact that sometimes God calls us to say things as His ambassadors that may cost us our very lives. Yet we must also remember that the Bible encourages us to walk in wisdom toward outsiders (Colossians 4:5) and also to be wise as serpents but harmless as doves (Matthew 10:16). That includes speaking the message of the Gospel in a way that it will receive the greatest possible acceptance. This perspective is consistent with the way Jesus and His disciples sought to reach others with the Good News.

Some may ask, How do we determine how deep we can go in our conversation with others about Christ and yet not burn our bridges? Experience has taught us that the more opportunities we have to interact with unsaved friends, family members, or coworkers in social or work settings, the more prudent it is to follow the dictum "less is more." However, in those situations where we may have little opportunity to continue the conversation at another time, sometimes "more is more." Sometimes it is more prudent to go further in spiritual dialogue with others, especially if we feel prompted by the Holy Spirit and may not have another chance to share with them the Good News of Christ.

You've probably heard it said, "You may be the only Bible that some people ever read." With unsaved family members it's more important for them to see the Good News in our life before they ever hear it on our lips.

Allowing Others to Surface the Truth for Themselves by Asking Probing Questions

For pre-evangelism to be fruitful, it also means that in certain situations, we will need to ask our nonbelieving friends questions that allow them *to surface the truth for themselves* and thereby help them evaluate the strength of their beliefs. We live in a world in which people are reluctant to be told what is true, but they may be willing to see for themselves, as in a mirror,[14] the inconsistencies in what they believe. When this takes place, we can help them to build bridges to the Gospel, based in part on our mutually shared beliefs (1 Corinthians 9:22).

Jesus Is Our Example to Follow in Asking Questions. Asking probing questions is not a unique approach in evangelism. If we look at the New Testament, it is clear that Jesus and His disciples used different kinds of questions and approaches depending on the audience they were addressing. So Jesus was not only the greatest teacher ever, He was also the greatest apologist who knew how to use questions effectively in His conversations with others.[15] In fact, the Gospels record over 200 questions that Jesus asked. He was a master at asking questions.

Jesus also knew the value of allowing others to surface the truth for themselves. When He spoke to the woman at the well (John 4), He did not tell her "turn or you will burn." Instead, He asked her thought-provoking questions and piqued her curiosity. He told her that if she drank of the water that He gives, she would never be thirsty again (John 4:14).

Jesus knew that sometimes it was best not to tell people things so directly. Many times He told parables that not all were able to understand clearly (Matthew 13:11-13). He did this to create a greater spiritual hunger in those who were interested. He also knew that it is not always best to share all that we know. Toward the end of His ministry He told His disciples, "I have much more to say to you, more than you can now bear" (John 16:12). We may want to say many things to our nonbelieving friends about Jesus, but they may be able to bear only a little at a time of what we want to tell them.

Jesus and His Disciples Are Examples to Follow in Finding Common Ground. Jesus and His disciples also understood the value of knowing the perspective of those they were speaking to and then building bridges to the truth from that perspective. For example, when Jesus healed the paralytic in Mark 2:1-13, He knew that the Pharisees understood that *God alone can forgive sins* (vv. 6-7). Knowing this, Jesus said to them,

"But that you may know that the Son of Man has authority on earth to forgive sins…" He said to the paralytic, "I tell you, get up, take your mat and go home" (vv. 10-11).

The apostle Paul had the same understanding in his interactions with others. In Acts 28:23, Paul's approach to the Jews and the God-fearing Greeks was to help them see that Jesus' life and death was the fulfillment of the Old Testament Scriptures, which they had already accepted. Yet, when Paul spoke to the Epicureans (atheists) and Stoics (pantheists) in Acts 17:22-29, he used another approach. Here, he spoke first about their false beliefs about God and not about the person of Christ. Likewise, when speaking to polytheists (in Acts 14) he had another strategy, beginning with nature and reasoning back to its creator. So, it is important that we choose the best approach to gain a hearing with those we are trying to reach (1 Corinthians 9:22).

The Bottom Line About Using Pre-evangelism in Our Evangelism

The more pre-evangelism we do, the more opportunities we will have to do evangelism. And the more opportunities we have to share the Gospel, the greater the likelihood that more people will come to know Christ. Therefore, the more pre-evangelism we do, the greater the likelihood that more people will come to Christ! We need to put new wine in new wineskins to reach the skeptics, pluralists, and relativists of our day (Matthew 9:17).

This combined approach of asking questions, creating interest, and building bridges to the cross is at the heart of pre-evangelism. It attempts to loosen the soil of people's minds and hearts by surfacing uncertainties in their beliefs and creating a desire to hear more about Jesus. If we buy into this approach, we will also need to consider the important role that Christian evidences should play in our evangelism,[16] even as our world and unfortunately some Christians move further from accepting any kind of objective truth.[17]

Sometimes we may not get far in helping people surface their uncertainties and creating a greater interest to hear more. However, we need to plant seeds about Jesus in our dialogue with nonbelievers today and leave it in God's sovereign hands that they could yield fruit tomorrow. We must continue to do our part every day to help our nonbelieving friends take one step closer to Jesus Christ (1 Corinthians 3:6).

May God help all of us to understand, like the men of Issachar, the times in which we live, and may He give us the strength and courage to make the sacrifices necessary to equip ourselves so that we will know how to do pre-evangelism in the New Millennium.

Reflection

1. Ask yourself: Who do I know that I've had trouble witnessing to in the past using a more traditional approach to evangelism? What could I do differently in future conversations based on what I learned in this chapter (see John 16:12)?

2. If I truly believed that engaging others in pre-evangelistic conversation is necessary in today's world, I would _____

_____

_____

Application

1. Determine the three people you most want to reach with the Gospel (this could be family members, friends, neighbors, coworkers, classmates). Write their names under the space provided in the appendix 1 worksheet. Ask God for wisdom (James 1:5) to know how to build pre-evangelistic bridges in your conversations with them over the next few months.

2. Pray for the three people you identified in the previous question, asking God to move in their lives in a way that creates greater spiritual openness. Ask God also for sensitivity

in using daily conversations in ways that create greater openness for spiritual dialogue.

3. Pray for God to strengthen you to be a positive and consistent witness to the people in your life; pray that Christ would be evident in your life as you interact with them day by day (Philippians 1:14).

4. Pray for open doors to plant seeds of the Gospel of Christ with those around you as you go about your daily routine, and for God to give you the wisdom and strength to be a good witness in how you speak God's truth to them (Acts 14:1). Meditate on Colossians 4:2-6.

Chapter 2

Introduction to Conversational Evangelism

A few years ago, on my way to a conference in the U.S., I sat on the plane next to a person who was rather chatty. Seeking to be a positive witness, I tried to strike up a spiritual conversation with him. To my surprise, I found out that not only was he a Mormon, but he was also the head teaching Mormon in his area of Washington State. I could have asked him some confrontational questions such as, "How can you believe in Mormonism when Joseph Smith made prophecies that didn't come true?" I decided instead to ask him nonthreatening questions and allow him to process the questions I raised and the concerns I had.

So I asked, "Can you help me understand something about Mormonism that seems confusing to me?"

"Sure," he said.

"How can Mormons believe in an infinite progression of gods?"

"What do you mean?"

"Don't you believe that Elohim god was once a man and that there were other gods before him and that there was a progression of gods before them? Don't you have to start with one God somewhere?"

I explained to him from a philosophical point of view the problems with an infinite regress in causes, and I could see that he was caught a little off guard. Much of our conversation for the rest of the flight proceeded in the following way: I would raise a question about Mormonism, and he would hesitate, unsure what to say. After several minutes of this, I asked if he knew of anyone who could answer my questions. He paused for a moment and then said he knew a professor at Brigham Young University who might be able to.

Here was one of the head teaching Mormons in Washington State, and he knew of only one person who *might* be able to answer my questions. I could see that our friendly but intellectually penetrating dialogue had an effect on him.

I further explained to him that I was a seeker of truth and that if I was wrong about what I believe, I wanted him to show me where I erred because I didn't want to believe what is false. "After all," I said, "the apostle Paul said in 1 Corinthians 15:14 that if Christ didn't really rise from the dead, our faith is in vain."

Just before he departed the plane he told me how much he enjoyed our conversation. Then he said something that took me by surprise. He said I was the first Protestant Christian who had talked to him about religious issues that was (in his words) "not in his face."

Since that moment, I have become more and more convinced that as Christians, we need a different approach to evangelism, especially if we desire to win those who are not the enemy but are themselves victims of the enemy (2 Corinthians 4:4). We need to learn how to tactfully ask probing questions of our nonbelieving friends in a way that allows them to surface the truth for themselves and create the curiosity to want to hear more about Jesus. This kind of encounter reflects the heart of the Conversational Evangelism approach.[1]

An Overview of Four Types of Conversational Engagements in Pre-Evangelism

Conversational Evangelism consists of four major kinds of conversations we want to have with our nonbelieving friends: Hearing Conversations, Illuminating Conversations, Uncovering Conversations, and Building Conversations (we'll explore these in detail in the chapters that follow). These are the main ingredients to the Conversational

Evangelism model. Developing skills in these four types of conversations could play an important role in building a bridge to the Gospel with our friends, especially those skeptics, pluralists, and postmodernists of our day (John 8:32).

Each of these conversational types corresponds to the roles we need to play in our non-Christian friends' lives: that of a *musician, artist, archaeologist,* and *builder.*[2] As a *musician,* we want to listen more carefully and also we want to hear the sour notes people are singing to us. As an *artist,* we want to paint a picture using questions to help others see themselves in a true light. As an *archaeologist,* we want to dig up their history and find the real barriers that are chaining them down. As a *builder,* we want to build a bridge to the Gospel.

Understanding how to have these four kinds of conversations with our nonbelieving friends as we fill these four key roles is important if we're going to help others take steps toward Christ.

Jesus' Use of Questions in the Gospels

Some may consider this a unique approach, but it is consistent with what Jesus did in ministering to others. Observe the following examples of His use of questions:

Matthew 12:9-14. Jesus entered a synagogue and saw a man with a shriveled hand. The Jewish leaders were looking for a reason to accuse Jesus of working on the Sabbath and thus breaking the fourth commandment, so they asked Him, "Is it lawful to heal on the Sabbath?" (v. 12). Jesus said to them, "If any of you has a sheep and it falls into a pit on the Sabbath, will you not take hold of it and lift it out? How much more valuable is a man than a sheep! Therefore it is lawful to do good on the Sabbath" (vv. 11-12). By His question Jesus showed that men would be willing to work to rescue a distressed sheep on the Sabbath. And if they were willing to rescue an animal, how much more should they be willing to restore a man who is created in the image of God.

John 7:21-24. Jesus defends His healing on the Sabbath by asking a question of the Jews: "Now if a child can be circumcised on the Sabbath so that the law of Moses may not be broken, why are you angry with me for healing the whole man on the Sabbath?" (v. 23). The Old Testament Law required a boy to be circumcised eight days after his birth. If that day happened to fall on the Sabbath, the child was still to be circumcised on that day to avoid breaking the law. Why then was it wrong for Jesus to heal a person and make him whole on the Sabbath?

John 10:22-41. Here Jesus is accused of blasphemy, for He has declared Himself to be God's Son. Jesus points to the testimony of His miracles and asks His opponents, "I have shown you many great miracles from the Father. For which of these do you stone me?" (v. 32). The Jewish crowd is infuriated by this claim and says, "We are not stoning you for any of these, but for blasphemy, because you, a mere man, claim to be God" (v. 33). Again Jesus answered with a question (based on Psalm 82): Israel's appointed judges were called "gods" not because they were divine beings, but because they were God's spokesmen speaking for God. Jesus asked, if these men could be called gods because of the authority delegated to them, how much more could Jesus be called the Son of God after performing all the great miracles He performed, thus demonstrating God's authority was upon Him?

Matthew 7:11. Jesus said, "If you, then, though you are evil, know how to give good gifts to your children, how much more will your Father in heaven give good gifts to those who ask him!" This statement contains an *a fortiori* (with the greater force) argument in hypothetical form: 1) If evil men know how to give good gifts to their children, then how much more does God. 2) Evil men do know how to give good gifts to their children. 3) Therefore, even more so, God knows how to give good gifts to His children.

Matthew 22:41-46. Here Jesus asked a question that stopped all questions from His opponents. They accepted the Messiah as the Son of David but not the Son of God. But Jesus said: 1) If David by the Holy Spirit called the Messiah his "Lord" (Psalm 110:1), then the Messiah must have been more than the mere son of David (i.e., a descendant of David). 2) David did call the Messiah "Lord." 3) Therefore, the Messiah was more than a descendant of David; He was also David's Lord (i.e., God).

Luke 6:6-11. Jesus healed a man with a withered hand on the Sabbath.

But before He did, He asked the Pharisees: "Is it lawful on the Sabbath to do good?" (v. 9). They knew it was. So His argument took this form: 1) It is lawful to do good on the Sabbath. 2) Healing a man's hand is good. 3) Therefore, it is lawful to heal a man's hand on the Sabbath.

His question-asking logic was invincible.

The Art of Asking Questions in a Nonthreatening Way

When we learn how to ask probing but nonthreatening questions, it allows others to surface the truth for themselves, rather than us trying to tell them what they should believe. Many non-Christians don't even like the idea that Christians still believe in absolute truth. Some may even consider us arrogant and intolerant for doing so. This makes it more necessary for us to engage others in low-key spiritual dialogue if we're ever going to create an environment where they are open to hear what we have to say about Jesus.

Creating an interest in spiritual dialogue is not an easy art to master. It is important that we learn not only how to ask our friends the right kinds of questions in a way that allows them to surface the truth for themselves, but also that we phrase our questions in the least threatening way possible. In order to do this we need to keep the following three things in mind:

1. ask questions in a way that *surfaces uncertainty* about their own perspective

2. *minimize their defensiveness*

3. *create in them a curiosity* to want to hear more

Trying to surface uncertainty in others' beliefs while minimizing their defensiveness is not an easy task. Any attempt we make to point out discrepancies can potentially make them very defensive. This is especially true when witnessing to the skeptics, pluralists, and postmodernists of our day.

We should take a hint from how we should speak to our spouse or other loved ones when we're having a disagreement. We shouldn't point out every little thing they say or do that doesn't make sense to us. That would just make them defensive and cause them to push away from us emotionally. Instead, we should gently express our *major* concerns, highlighting those areas of disagreement that seem most important to us, and hope they see these as well.

In the same way, when witnessing to others, wisdom sometimes requires us to point out just a few key things we would like others to think about. We shouldn't dump our truckload all at once. One ex-Jehovah's Witness has come to a similar conclusion: "If the Christian warrior corners an individual Jehovah's Witness and lets him have it with both barrels in rapid fire succession, the result is likely to be disappointing."[3]

Jesus' Example in Mastering the Art of Asking Questions

After many hours of teaching His disciples, Jesus knew they could absorb only a little at a time. He said in John 16:12, "I have much more to say to you, more than you can now bear." Likewise, while we want to tell others many things about Jesus, they can bear only so much at one time.

That's one reason why it's essential to ask penetrating questions about others' beliefs. David Baker says, "A person can close his ears to facts he does not want to hear, but if a pointed question causes him to form the answer in his own mind, he cannot escape the conclusion—because it's a conclusion that he reached himself."[4]

Uncovering Real Barriers

We want to do more than deconstruct unbelievers' belief systems.[5] We also want to discover the real barriers that keep them from believing in Christ. The intellectual sounding questions unbelievers direct at Christians are often a smoke screen to keep the message of the Gospel at bay. We need to determine if their questions or concerns are based on intellectual barriers, emotional barriers, volitional barriers, or some combination of the three.

Uncovering the barriers can help your nonbelieving friends take steps toward Christ. Without removing those barriers, we may find it difficult for others even to hear our simple Gospel message. Once we help someone see their inconsistencies of belief and uncover their real barriers, we can then help them to take positive steps toward Christ.

Building a Strategy for Sharing the Gospel

After we have engaged people in these ways, we can then develop a strategy for how to most effectively reach them with the Gospel. Our goal here is to determine the most effective way to dialogue with others so that "many will believe" (Acts 14:1). We need to assess what will be the most helpful bridge we can construct that will encourage others to want to know more about our Jesus.

To accomplish this takes some strategic planning on our part.[6] It is especially important that we take time to develop a strategy for building a bridge to the Gospel over an extended period of time. We need to think about long-term interaction with nonbelievers, not the traditional one-time Gospel presentation. In short, our pre-evangelism must be intentional and strategic if we're going to have a maximum impact on those we're trying to reach for Christ.

An effective approach then in doing pre-evangelism with those influenced by postmodern thought is to first *listen carefully to them*. Only then are we ready to *hear the discrepancies* in their beliefs. Once we uncover those discrepancies or contradictions, we want to shine a light on them so our friends clearly see them. We do this when we ask thought-provoking questions and allow the truth to surface naturally.

After we carefully illuminate the discrepancies, then we want to *uncover the surface barriers* to get down to the real barriers that prevent others from seriously considering Christ.

Then we need to *build a bridge* to the Gospel. Our ultimate goal is to remove obstacles so that others can take one step closer to Christ each day (1 Corinthians 3:6).

Once our non-Christian friends are convinced of Christ's credentials and of their need for Him, then we can share the Gospel and invite them to trust in Christ. Pre-evangelism will have led to the opportunity for direct evangelism.

Key Components of This Pre-evangelism Model

Eight main ingredients make up this pre-evangelistic approach: 1) active listening, 2) positive deconstructionism,[7] 3) a questioning approach that allows others to surface the truth, 4) the boomerang principle,[8] which involves removing the burden of proof from us to them, 5) determining the real barriers to the Gospel, 6) finding common ground, 7) a strategy for building a bridge to the Gospel (both intelletual and heart bridges), and 8) a basic knowledge of the Christian faith and what makes Jesus unique. The importance of mastering these key elements will become evident as we explain each one in more detail in the following chapters.

Effective Use of This Pre-evangelism Model

This model for pre-evangelism should not be reduced to following a formula. So although we want to always start with step one and focus on listening to what others really believe and hearing their sour notes, where we go next depends on our sensitivity to the Holy Spirit's leading as He gives us a greater awareness of the needs of the person we're attempting to reach.

For example, after listening to someone for a period of time and having a good idea of that person's worldview and the sour notes it entails, sometimes, rather than going to step two and asking him questions to surface the discrepancies in his beliefs, it's best to go to step three and try to dig up underlying barriers. Sometimes the barriers are such a problem that we may not get an opportunity to help nonbelievers see anything wrong with their current beliefs and help them uncover the truth about Christianity until those barriers are removed.

As you can see, using this model effectively takes a lot of wisdom and discernment from the Holy Spirit. In this way, learning to engage others in pre-evangelism is more of an art than a science.

Pre-evangelism, like discipleship, is also more caught than taught. As you practice pre-evangelism as a way of life, you will begin to "catch" how to engage people in ways that lead to more fruitful discussions and greater opportunities for direct evangelism.

When you first learned to ride a bicycle, you may have skinned your knees a few times before you got the hang of it. Similarly, your first attempts to do pre-evangelism may seem to be a failure. You may feel as though you said all the wrong things at all the wrong times and brought up all the wrong steps in the wrong order. Yet as pre-evangelism becomes more and more a way of life, you will begin to catch how to engage others in a way that leads to more fruitful discussions and greater openness for direct evangelism.

Finding the Balance Between Surfacing Uncertainty and Creating an Interest in Jesus

To use this model effectively, we also need to find a balance in creating uncertainty in others' beliefs while creating more interest in what we have to say about Jesus. Merely deconstructing someone's beliefs can make him increasingly defensive, forming a barrier against hearing anything we have to say about Jesus. Therefore, we need to remain reliant on the Holy Spirit as we practice the fine art of knowing what to say, how much to say, and when to say those things that will gently surface uncertainty.

We must learn the skill of talking to non-Christians in a way that makes them feel *uncertain* about their beliefs and what they are basing their life on, and yet minimizes their discomfort with us so that they want to continue the conversation. It is part of what Paul challenged us to do when he said, "Be wise in the way you act toward outsiders; make the most of every opportunity. Let your conversation be always full of grace, seasoned with salt, so that you may know how to answer everyone" (Colossians 4:5-6).

Advantages to Using the Conversational Evangelism Approach

We need to remind ourselves of a number of advantages to learning how to use this pre-evangelistic approach so that we don't get disheartened and forget why we're doing this.

First, this approach can be especially effective in witnessing to those who are indifferent, skeptical, or hostile to the claims of Christ because it allows them to explore the cracks in their foundation in the least threatening way possible. This may encourage them to critically reconsider their beliefs. As a result, they may become more open to hear what we believe as Christians, and why we believe it.

Second, we do not need to have a thorough knowledge of apologetics (though it would be helpful) to effectively use this approach. By merely listening to what our nonbelieving friends say, we can discern the religious terminology they use that may need clarification, which may in turn help them to think more clearly about their own beliefs. It may also open doors to move conversations from pre-evangelism to direct evangelism.

Third, even with very little apologetics knowledge, we may learn to surface the discrepancies in others' beliefs by merely listening carefully to what they say about what they believe and hear their sour notes. We can then ask thought-provoking questions (based on their stated beliefs) to help them think more clearly about those beliefs.

Fourth, this approach also encourages us to find that right balance between cognitive and noncognitive elements in evangelism. Sometimes the real obstacles are not primarily intellectual but emotional or spiritual, and we need to develop our sensitivity to the Holy Spirit and ask for wisdom to discern what kind of approach would be most helpful with our friends.

Fifth, we still may be able to make spiritual progress with people we don't consider to be our friends provided there is openness on their part to continue the spiritual dialogue.

Sixth, it also provides a methodology for doing pre-evangelism that can easily be taught to others using the roles of the musician, artist, archaeologist, and builder. The Conversational Evangelism model is a transferable concept not meant to replace other good evangelistic tools, such as the *Four Spiritual Laws* or the Navigators' *Bridge Illustration* or *Evangelism Explosion*, but to supplement that training. Today's evangelist needs to see pre-evangelism as an essential part of his training for evangelism.

Learning the Mechanics of Pre-evangelism

One problem in using a pre-evangelistic approach is that it can seem mechanical and impersonal. Some of us had a similar experience using a Gospel tract for the first time. Yet after a while, we were able to combine the presentation of the Gospel in the tract with our personal style of communication in such a seamless way that we no longer needed to use a tract to share the Good News with others.

The same can be true of learning to do pre-evangelism. It may seem impersonal and mechanical at first. But after we use this approach for a while we will know better how to engage others in a way that's more natural to our personality and that brings about greater openness to spiritual dialogue.

Or to change the illustration, some of us may remember how difficult it was to learn to drive a car with a manual transmission. But after some practice, driving with a clutch became a natural part of the driving experience. In a similar way, once we learn the mechanics involved in Conversational Evangelism, we may be able to integrate it seamlessly into our evangelistic approach such that our pre-evangelistic encounters lead to more open doors for direct evangelism.

The Important Role of the Holy Spirit in Evangelism

Before we get into the details of this pre-evangelism model, it is critical that we understand the vital role the Holy Spirit plays in empowering us to make a difference in people's lives. He does this in several ways.

First, He empowers us to speak in a way that makes a difference (Acts 14:1). Luke records that Paul and his disciples "spoke so effectively that a great number of Jews and Gentiles believed." Yet Paul declares his strong reliance on the work of the Holy Spirit when he says his message and preaching "were not in persuasive words of wisdom, but in demonstration of the Spirit and of power" (1 Corinthians 2:4 NASB). The Holy Spirit was working behind the scenes to convict others using the words Paul spoke.

So our words also can have a powerful impact on people's lives if they are empowered by the Spirit. The more persuasive our words, the more the Holy Spirit can use them to affect others. In short, apologetic pre-evangelism can lead the horse to the water, but only the Holy Spirit can persuade him to drink.

Second, only the Holy Spirit can convict a person of sin. Jesus said, "When [the Holy Spirit] comes, he will convict the world of guilt in regard to sin and righteousness and judgment" (John 16:8). Apologetics never saved anyone, even the best of pre-evangelistic apologetics. Only God can save. At best, apologetics is only a tool the Holy Spirit may use in bringing a person to Christ.

Third, only the Holy Spirit can convert a person from sinner to saved. As Jesus told Nicodemus, "I tell you the truth, no one can enter the kingdom of God unless he is born of water and the Spirit. Flesh gives birth to flesh, but the Spirit gives birth to spirit" (John 3:5-6).

Fourth, the Holy Spirit empowers us to live godly lives, which helps make us a better channel through which the Spirit can work. Paul's attitude during his imprisonment encouraged many "to speak the word of God more courageously and fearlessly" (Philippians 1:14). Paul's life was powerful evidence to many that God is real and that Jesus really is the Messiah. So we not only must articulate the truths of the Gospel persuasively, but we also have an obligation to live holy, attractive lives.

This is especially important in reaching those influenced by postmodern thinking. People today don't care how much we know until they know how much we care and feel like they can trust us. Therefore, we must ask God to empower us to be "wise in the way [we] act" (Colossians 4:5), especially toward "outsiders" (those outside the faith). They are watching us and listening carefully to our conversations to see if what we say matches how we behave. Our actions and attitudes are the only reference points they have to gauge the authenticity of what we say we believe. Consequently, what we say and do either authenticates or invalidates our faith.

We must constantly remind ourselves that we are just the instruments God desires to use. Paul tells us that "God chose the foolish things of the world to shame the wise; God chose the weak things of the world to shame the strong" (1 Corinthians 1:27). You and I are only ordinary people that God takes pleasure in using in extraordinary ways to reveal His truth to a lost and dying world. We should not feel pressure to produce results, because ultimately the Holy Spirit does the work, and we are just His instruments. Our job is only to be responsible to obey what God has called us to do, whether we feel qualified to do it or not.

God is not so much concerned about our ability, but our availability and willingness to be used as His instruments. Consequently, it is important that the Holy Spirit empower us to speak the truth and to live the truth. Both are important if we're going to reach this generation of skeptics, pluralists, and postmodernists.

Reflection

1. Why do you think the Mormon I talked with felt open to chat with me even when he discovered I was a non-Mormon and he suspected that we disagreed on so much?

2. What kinds of things could someone have said to him that could have caused him to get defensive and cut off any more spiritual dialogue? How can you and I avoid running into spiritual roadblocks in future conversations with our friends or acquaintances?

3. Have you ever had an experience where someone with a different belief than yours seemed to enjoy your spiritual conversation with them? What things might have kept that person continuing the dialogue with you?

4. Think back to the first time you learned how to present the Gospel using a simple script. You might have felt at one time that you would never be able to share the Gospel in a natural, unforced way. What changed to allow you to feel more comfortable explaining the Gospel to people?

5. What might motivate you to learn a pre-evangelistic approach, even if it seemed difficult, impersonal, and mechanical at first (1 Chronicles 12:32)?

6. Complete this statement: Knowing that I am just God's

instrument helps me in witnessing by _____
_____(1 Corinthians 1:27).

7. Review the examples in this chapter about Jesus and His use of questions. What examples stand out in your mind and why?

8. Think of one situation you may have found yourself in recently while talking with friends where you were able to use questions to help them in their spiritual journey. What was it about your questions that helped them?

Application

1. Read the summary chart in appendix 2, steps 1-4, which gives the big picture of the Conversational Evangelism model. As you go through the chapters of this book, refresh your understanding of each point of the model by looking back at the chart. This will help you absorb more quickly into your memory the important concepts of the model, which could help you as you develop your top three list (appendix 1).

2. Complete this statement of personal commitment: In light of my greater understanding of how Jesus used questions, this week in my witness to my friends, I will

_____.

3. Complete this statement of personal commitment: For me to speak more persuasively to my friends (Acts 14:1) and in dependency on God (John 6:65), I will begin to

_____.

Chapter 3

Learning the Role
of the Musician

Interviewer: Do you think it really matters what we believe?

Student: Yes, I think people base their lives off of their beliefs. So you have to have something to follow.

Interviewer: How do you personally determine right or wrong?

Student: I think the standard varies from person to person, and I think maybe majority rules. The world kind of said _____ Hitler, and that is what we did.

Interviewer: Okay, so if you think majority rule determines what is right and wrong, what about back in times of slavery when we thought it was okay to have slaves?

Student: True, man, it's life philosophy all over again. Uh...I think there is going to be an example to contradict every situation. There is not a set answer to that question. So it just varies from person to person.

Interviewer: So there is no such thing as absolutes?

Student: Nah.

Interviewer: Are you absolutely certain?

Student: Yes.

Why Developing Listening Skills Is So Important in Evangelism

In order to challenge nonbelievers to consider the person of Christ, it is increasingly useful to learn how to engage them in pre-evangelism. This requires us to improve our listening skills and to allow them to surface the truth for themselves rather than for us to proclaim it to them. We must discover the kinds of questions that will surface any uncertainty about their own perspective in order to challenge them to think more carefully through their beliefs. This may in turn create more openness on their part to hear what we have to say about Christ.

Unfortunately, we do not always hear what our friends of other religious perspectives are saying, which makes it difficult to determine what they actually believe. We forget to listen first to their questions and concerns. As a result, we may not have the right information to ask the questions that will prompt interest in what we have to say. We may end up asking questions that do not surface the core issues important to our friend and that also cause unnecessary defensiveness, cutting off any future dialogue. If we do not care enough about a person to really listen, they will likely pick up on this. This too will have a dampening effect on our relationship with them and our future interactions.

To be more effective in reaching others, we will have to work harder on really listening to people to know what they believe so we can know better how to reach them. Everything begins with careful listening.

Good conversation begins with good listening. Hence, the first step in Conversational Evangelism is to *hear what others actually believe* and then detect discrepancies in their viewpoint. But before we detect any discrepancies, we need to first focus our attention on *learning to be better listeners and hear them clearly.*

How many of us remember as a child our mother saying to us, "Are you listening to me?" All too often we did not hear what our mother was saying. In the same way, we do not always hear what our nonbelieving friends are saying to us. James 1:19 says, "My dear brothers, take note of this: Everyone should be quick to listen, slow to speak and slow to become angry."

Listening Is Critical in Witnessing to Those in a Postmodern World

Listening carefully is especially important because people of different faiths often don't hold their religious views consistently and even mix and match views. A taxi driver once confessed that he was a Buddhist, but when we asked whether he was a devout Buddhist, he said he was more of a "free thinker." On another occasion a self-professed Muslim said he thought that all the religions basically teach the same thing, a position clearly contrary to the teachings of Islam. Therefore it is extremely important that we learn to listen without forming any preconceptions about a non-Christian's beliefs so that we can better understand what that person actually believes and not just take at face value the religious label he gives us.

Another important reason to listen carefully is that people we witness to often use familiar Christian terminology, but if we listen more closely, we may discover that these familiar words have different meanings than our own. It is important that we first learn how to really listen to what others are saying without trying to hear what we want to hear or assume the terms they use carry the same connotation.

At times our inability to really listen to others may be due in part to our own misapplication of the biblical injunction "to give an answer" (1 Peter 3:15). We may fall into the trap of quickly giving an answer (sometimes any answer!) in order to not look foolish or to portray some amount of confidence. We may also have to break the bad habit of focusing on what we want to say next rather than listening to what the other person is saying. In doing so, we may misread them and miss hearing something that could have been helpful in our dialogue with them. We will find it difficult to offer a relevant answer or even ask a penetrating question to help our friends surface the truth for themselves if we haven't taken the time to really hear them and understand their beliefs.

One helpful suggestion for increasing our listening skills is to practice the art of reflection—that is, to "reflect back" what others say to us. Attempt to paraphrase what they say and ask if we have understood them. This is similar to what we might do to improve our communication with our spouse. We could respond, "What I hear you saying is… Is that accurate?"

The Practical Value of Increasing Our Listening Skills

Hearing is such an important step in pre-evangelism for three additional reasons. First, it helps us better connect with others. People feel appreciated when we understand their concerns and show patience in our dialogue with them. Second, it helps to put the other person at ease. If people sense you are genuinely trying to understand them, they may be less defensive and let down their guard to engage in honest dialogue. Third, as we develop good listening habits in our conversations with our nonbelieving friends, we may be able to identify some inconsistency in their beliefs that will then allow us to ask them just the right kind of question that would lead to further dialogue. This may also help to uncover the nature of their barriers to Christ, whether intellectual, emotional, or spiritual. The Bible reminds us of the importance of listening carefully, for "he who answers before listening—that is his folly and his shame" (Proverbs 18:13).

So in the Conversational Evangelism model, "Hearing Conversations" is always the first step in our pre-evangelistic engagements. Our goal is to listen for clues to what our non-Christian friends really believe deep in their hearts.

Hearing the Sour Notes

As we listen to others, we want to *hear the sour notes they sing to us.* What do I mean by sour notes? Well, have you ever heard someone singing off-key? You may not be sure if that person's pitch is too high or too low, but it is clear that something doesn't sound right. In the same way, in our conversations with our nonbelieving friends, we may hear things that just do not sound right. They may sound to us like sour notes. If someone says, "There are absolutely no absolutes," does this not sound like a sour note?

One sour note voiced more and more by our postmodern friends is, "Language cannot adequately convey meaning, and I really mean it!" Hear the sour note? Another statement heard more and more frequently is, "Reality as we know it is not real. Life is merely a social construct." For those impacted by Eastern thinking, an example of a sour note is when someone who claims to be a devout Buddhist also expresses a strong desire to win the lottery. To desire anything goes against the central principles of what Buddha taught.

One of the most common sour notes we hear today is the idea that "all religious views are essentially true." Yet not all views of reality can be true, because a point in every direction is no point at all. If you are pointing in every direction, you are not pointed in any one specific direction. If you embrace *everything,* you stand for *nothing.* To proclaim that all views are true is to be illogical and stand for no particular truth. In reality you believe in nothing!

Furthermore, not all views can be right because some are contradictory. Either Jesus is the only "way and the truth and the life" (John 14:6) or He is not the only way and the truth and the life. But He cannot be both.

There are also contradictory truth claims regarding "salvation." Christianity claims that salvation comes by faith alone in Christ alone. Islam claims that salvation comes by belief in Allah, his prophet Muhammad, and good works. Hinduism claims that it is by overcoming karma and incarnations with good works. Buddhism claims it comes about by cessation of desire through the eight-fold path. All these views of salvation cannot be right. So it is important that we tune our ears to hear the sour notes in the beliefs of those we have regular contact with, which may provide us the right questions to ask them.

Some May Not Hear Their Sour Notes Clearly

Sour notes come in all sizes and shapes. Some are more easily identifiable than others. For example, some may think that the statement "God is so far beyond us that we really cannot know anything about Him" does not seem to be a sour note. But when we reflect upon the statement, we realize that the claim that we cannot know anything about God *is itself* a statement about what God is like.

When atheistic scientists such as Richard Dawkins insist that the universe could have evolved from matter and energy, this may not seem like a sour note. But once you allow the high improbability (from a scientific point of view) of any life to exist, you have only three options: either that life always existed, or it came to be from nothing, or it came to be by something that is eternal. Now if that life form is contingent,[1] you have only two options: either it came from something or it came from nothing and by nothing. Yet what reasonable person would believe that it is more likely that the personal came from the impersonal, or that the immaterial came from the material, or that something actually was produced from nothing? Certainly this is not part of our uniform experience upon which scientific principles are derived. Consequently this belief is also a sour note.

Uncovering Discrepancies Is an Important Role in Reaching Others

Listening for sour notes in our conversations with others is an important concept found in the New Testament. In fact, God thinks so highly of correct reasoning that one of the qualifications for an elder in the church is that he be able to "refute those who contradict" (Titus 1:9 NASB). To contradict literally means to say yes and no at the same time and in the same sense. The apostle Paul points out that our message of the cross cannot contain contradictory beliefs. Paul said, "But as surely as God is faithful, our message to you is not 'Yes' and 'No' " (2 Corinthians 1:18). It is important to God that our beliefs not be contradictory. We must be able to reason correctly and listen carefully to detect when someone says things that contradict. We need to hear these sour notes.

What would you think if someone said that his wife is pregnant and also not pregnant at the same time? Is this a meaningful statement? This is an example of a sour note because it is so out of tune with reality. We must tune our ears to these kinds of statements in our conversations with our nonbelieving friends.

We need to listen for at least four types of sour notes or discrepancies: *belief versus heart longing, belief versus behavior, belief versus belief,* and *illogical belief.* Let's look at each of these sour notes more specifically.

The Sour Note of Belief Versus Heart Longing

Belief versus heart longing is the discrepancy between a person's worldview and his heart longing. In our postmodern culture, there is a desperate longing, especially among young people, for a sense of belonging. They want to be a part of something bigger than themselves, yet their worldview does not allow for a sense of ultimate meaning and purpose for their life.

Sometime shortly after 9/11, a student confessed that he did not believe in an afterlife, either heaven or hell. Yet he did believe that the terrorists were somehow going to be responsible after this life for what they had done. While his worldview of atheism informed him otherwise, his heart's cry was that justice must be done! Another student confessed after 9/11 that he now realized that his life has to count for something. He could not just live a mundane life with a regular nine-to-five job. He wanted his life to be a part of something much greater. King Solomon reminds us that God "has also set eternity in the hearts of men; yet they cannot fathom what God has done from beginning to end" (Ecclesiastes 3:11).

All people, regardless of religion, share the heart longing to know and be known by others, and (though unknown to them) ultimately by God Himself. The famous French mathematician, philosopher, and physicist Blaise Pascal argued that humans have an internal emptiness they try to fill with all kinds of things and relationships, but the only One who can truly fill that emptiness is God.[2]

Even atheist Walter Kaufmann described man as a "God-intoxicated ape." But atheism cannot, on its own grounds, account for how this God-intoxication evolved in the human species. Former atheist and current head of the massive human genome project Francis Collins wrote:

> Why would such a universal and uniquely human hunger exist, if it were not connected to some opportunity for fulfillment? [C.S.] Lewis says it well: "Creatures are not born with desires unless satisfaction for desires exists. A baby feels hunger; well, there is such a thing as food. A duckling wants to swim: well, there is such a thing as water."...Why do we have a "God-shaped vacuum" in our hearts and minds unless it is meant to be fulfilled?[3]

Many world religions contain views that are inconsistent with the longings of people's hearts. Hinduism teaches that people can have a relationship only with an impersonal god. Yet the heart yearns for more than this. In Buddhism, the goal is to achieve a state of nirvana, which is an abstract nothingness. Yet reaching nirvana requires us to lose our personhood, which goes against the cry of our heart. Furthermore, nirvana can be attained only through a heavy burden of living according to rules and regulations that we can never completely keep.[4] Islamic teaching likewise betrays the heart's cry to have intimacy with God. Only through Christ can we find truly satisfying fulfillment for our heart's cry. Ravi Zacharias reminds us,

> What oxygen is to the brain, Jesus is to our hearts. He satisfies our deepest longings unlike anything else...If we were to list all of our hungers, we might be surprised at how many legitimate hungers we have. We hunger for truth, love, knowledge, belonging, self-expression, justice, imagination, learning, and significance—to name a few. If we browse any library, or bookstore, we will soon realize that the vast psychological theories have emerged to describe each one of these hungers or needs. As important and right as those needs are, our need for Jesus is infinitely greater...Jesus put an exclamation point on His supreme place in our life. He who comes to me will never be hungry, and he who believes in me will never be thirsty (Jn. 6:35).[5]

An increasingly common sour note heard in the West is, "I believe that as long as my material needs are met, that is all that really matters." Yet there are times that all of us hunger for truth, love, knowledge, justice, and significance. In Buddhist teaching it is commonly understood that we can achieve a state of nirvana only if we let go of our identity. Yet in reality even a Buddhist would not desire to let go of his identity because to do so would mean losing all conscious awareness of who he is.

The Sour Note of Belief Versus Behavior

The *belief versus behavior* inconsistency shows itself in the disjunction between what people say they believe and how they live. In Galatians 2:11-21 the apostle Paul confronted Peter about his inconsistent behavior. Peter had been eating with Gentile Christians in Antioch, yet when certain Jews came from Jerusalem, he stopped doing so. So Paul rebuked him since his belief and his behavior did not line up.

In the same way, many people often do not live consistently with what they say they believe. Helping others to identify these cracks in their belief system could play an important part in building pre-evangelistic bridges to the Gospel.

A student on a college campus once confessed that he did not think Hitler's extermination of six million Jews was necessarily wrong. Rather than challenging his statement directly, I said, "It must be hard living your life that way, huh?" His body language made it clear that I had penetrated his defenses. My statement knocked the wind right out of his sail because on some level he realized that what he professed to believe could not really be lived out. One of the last things he said was, "Maybe someday I'll go back to church."

Another example of this discrepancy occurred in a conversation with my Buddhist auto mechanic. "Is it not true that one of the main goals of Buddhism is to stop desiring?" I asked him.

"Yes," he said.

"If one of the goals of Buddhism is to stop desiring, how as a parent did you stop desiring to have your children?"

After a few moments passed, he said, "That is a problem." Then he started telling me some of his other concerns about Buddhism. He believed one thing, but his actions were not consistent with his beliefs, which caused him to question his Buddhist beliefs.

When talking with a Muslim about religious matters, we will often ask, "Do you pray at least five times a day?"

Many will say no.

"If Muslims believe that to get to heaven their good works have to outweigh their bad deeds, and yet they don't keep the minimum requirement of praying at least five times a day, how can they ever hope to get to heaven?"

So identifying the discrepancies between nonbelievers' beliefs and their behavior can play an important role in surfacing the vulnerable areas of their faith.

Some additional examples of the sour notes of belief versus behavior are:

- "I believe in naturalistic evolution, yet I try to live a good life."
- "I treat others with respect, yet there is no such thing as right and wrong."
- "I don't believe in life after death, yet I believe that we need to respect our dead ancestors by burning incense and giving hell money for them during the hungry ghost festival" (common in certain parts of the East).

The Sour Note of Belief Versus Belief

Another sour note is *holding two or more mutually contradictory beliefs*. We see an example of this sour note in Acts 17:28-29. Paul, speaking to the Athenian philosophers, said, " 'For in him we live and move and have our being.' As some of your own poets have said, 'We are his offspring.' Therefore since we are God's offspring, we should not think that the divine being is like gold or silver or stone—an image made by man's design and skill."

Paul identified two major inconsistencies in their beliefs: they believed they created the gods made of gold, silver, or stone, yet they also believed that these gods had created them. Paul's underlying question here is: "Can both these views be true?" Now the Athenians responded to Paul in three different ways. Some said, "Paul, you are crazy." Others said, "We want to hear more." Still others actually responded by trusting Christ (Acts 17:32-34).

So the Holy Spirit can use a person's awareness of his conflicting beliefs to help him take one step closer to Jesus Christ and even lead him to accept Christ.

When we talk to students on college campuses, we have many opportunities to hear some of these discrepancies.

"Who is Jesus Christ?" I asked one student.

"Jesus was the Son of God," he said.

"Do you believe Jesus is in any sense your Savior?"

"Yes."

"Do you believe you'll be accountable for how you live your life?"

He agreed that he would.

"Do you think you can measure up?"

"Well, I'm a pretty good person…"

"Why do you need Jesus to save you if you can measure up?"

After a few moments he said, "I guess I don't measure up."

This admission was an important part of the pre-evangelism process. If we cannot get others to acknowledge that they do not measure up, what need is there (from their perspective) for Christ to save them?

On another occasion a college girl said she believed the Bible is reliable, but she also believed she must do good works to be saved. This, of course, is contrary to what Scripture teaches (Ephesians 2:8-9; Titus 3:5). These are just a few examples of the kinds of belief-versus-belief discrepancies we can hear if we would only tune our ears. Other examples of the sour note of belief versus belief are:

- "I believe there are things that are right and wrong that transcend culture, but I don't believe God exists."
- "I believe there is ultimate meaning and purpose to my life, but I also believe I'm an accidental by-product of nature."

- "I think it's wrong to do experiments on animals to improve the lives of humans, yet I believe it's okay to abort an unborn child" (a common one among postmodern nonbelievers).

- "I'm a Christian, but I'm not sure why Jesus had to die on the cross."

One example in Islam of this sour note is the statement that Muhammad is the last and greatest prophet and Jesus is merely a great prophet. Yet their own Qur'an acknowledges that Jesus was without sin (Sura 3:45-46; 19:19-21) and virgin born (Sura 3:47), and that Muhammad was sinful (Sura 40:55; 48:1-2) and not virgin born.

A common sour note among Hindus is the belief that "all humans are reincarnated after death, and if they are bad they will become an animal." But if reincarnation is true, how can we account for both the increase in crime and the increase in the human population?

The Sour Note of Illogical Belief

The last kind of sour note or discrepancy is *illogical belief.* This kind of inconsistency is not between two different beliefs but within a single belief. For example, the declaration that "there are absolutely no absolutes" is illogical, like sawing off the very branch of a tree that one is resting on.

In one of A.A. Milne's stories, Winnie-the-Pooh comes knocking on Mr. Rabbit's door and says, "Anybody home?" Mr. Rabbit doesn't want to open the door because he knows that if he does, Pooh will eat him out of house and home. So Mr. Rabbit says from behind the closed door, "Nobody home." Winnie-the-Pooh scratches his head and says, wait a minute, there has to be someone home to say there's nobody home. For Mr. Rabbit to say "Nobody is home" is not a meaningful statement.

I can say, "I cannot utter a word in English," but it is not meaningful because I have to use English to say it.

You might be surprised how many people make similar statements that fit this category. Here are some examples of illogical or self-defeating statements:

- "You should be skeptical about everything."
- "God is so far beyond us that we cannot really know anything about Him."
- "There is really no absolute truth."
- "Everything is relative."
- "You can't really know anything."
- "I know for sure you can't know anything for sure."
- "I am absolutely sure that you should not come to any conclusions about what is right or wrong."
- "Always avoid making absolute statements."
- "You should always be tolerant of people of different religious beliefs except those who are not tolerant."

To summarize this part of the Conversational Evangelism model, we begin by first *earnestly listening* to our nonbelieving friends to understand what they believe. Only then are we ready to hear the *sour notes* or discrepancies. These four discrepancies are: *Belief versus Heart Longing, Belief versus Behavior, Belief versus Belief,* and *Illogical Belief.*

Once we have identified these sour notes, we can help those making such statements see themselves and their beliefs in a truer light. This is an important part of the pre-evangelism process because many have little motivation to reconsider their perspective (and possibly consider the person of Christ) when they do not see the cracks in their foundational beliefs. We should incorporate this approach into our evangelistic methodology, especially since both Jesus and the apostle Paul used it effectively.

As we identify different sour notes in others' beliefs, we must not forget the importance of earnestly listening to them.

Next to relying on the guidance and power of the Holy Spirit, clearly understanding their beliefs is the first and most important step in the pre-evangelism process.

The Alleged Sour Notes in Christian Beliefs

Now some may ask, "But what about all the sour notes in Christianity? Aren't there sour notes in your beliefs just as there are in other beliefs?" In the spirit of fairness and to answer readers' genuine desire for answers, we discuss here a few of the more common challenges voiced of the Christian faith. Additional points of interest are covered in appendix 4.

The Alleged Sour Note of Science Against Creation

The biggest scientific obstacle for most unbelievers is that the Bible teaches that God created the universe and life. Yet modern science insists that it all happened by natural forces through evolutionary processes. Some have attempted to overcome this by claiming God created the universe, and then everything else evolved naturally. However, there are two problems with this. First, atheists will not even grant that God created the universe. Second, theistic evolution does not fit with the Genesis account of God directly creating every living thing after its own kind (Genesis 1:21), nor of the direct creation of Adam from dust and woman from Adam's rib.

However, this alleged sour note is not as sour as it seems. Many top scientists argue that the universe and life could not have arisen by purely natural causes. These include Albert Einstein, Sir Fred Hoyle, James Collins, and numerous others. Indeed, a major astrophysicist, Robert Jastrow, declares,

> Now we see how the astronomical evidence leads to a biblical view of the origin of the world. The details differ, but the essential elements in the astronomical and biblical accounts of Genesis are the same: the chain of events leading to man commence suddenly and sharply at a definite moment in time, in a flash of light and energy…The scientist's pursuit of the past ends in the moment of creation…This is an exceedingly strange development, unexpected by all but theologians. They have always accepted the word of the Bible: "In the beginning God created the heavens and the earth."[6]

While naturalistic scientists wish there to be a natural cause for everything, Jastrow affirms: "That there are what I or anyone would call supernatural forces at work is now, I think, a scientifically proven fact."[7]

The Sour Note About a First Cause

Another note that seems sour to many unbelievers is the idea of God as a First, uncaused Cause. It is argued that if every cause needs a cause, then so does God. However, this is based on a false premise. There is no law that says "Every *cause* needs a cause." The law of causality states only that "Every *effect* needs a cause." Only effects (or things reducible to effects) need causes.

Put another way, everything that has a beginning needs a Beginner. But every Beginner does not need a Beginner. For example, every sculpture (effect) needs a sculptor (cause), yet every sculptor (cause) does not need another sculptor (cause).

Even atheists once claimed (and some still do) that the universe had no cause because it is eternal. Well, if the universe can be uncaused because it is eternal (which it is not according to big bang cosmology), then why can't God be the uncaused first cause. Whatever is eternal has no Beginning Cause, and whatever is not eternal needs a Beginning Cause. However, since the evidence for the big bang argues that the universe is not eternal, then it follows that the universe is caused, but the Cause of the universe is not caused since it had no beginning.

The Sour Note Between Belief Versus Behavior Among Christians

One of the biggest barriers to Christianity heard over and over again from our nonbelieving friends is the hypocritical testimony of so-called Christians. Unfortunately, some have been turned off to the Christian message partly because of people who say they are followers of Christ but whose lives communicate a different story. Certainly if the power that raised Jesus from the dead is available to empower Christians to live transformed lives (Philippians 3:10), then the world should see something different in the lives of Christians. This was certainly true of Christians in the first century. We even have secular sources that confirm that Christians lived lives different from non-Christians.[8]

In the age in which we live, however, some who profess to be Christians have fallen into the world's perspective of living for themselves. That is why Scripture warns professing Christians to test themselves and determine whether they are really in the faith (2 Corinthians 13:5). Just because someone claims to be a Christian doesn't mean they are one.

Some of the things done in the name of Christ, such as the Crusades in the Middle Ages, were not things that Jesus Himself would always be pleased with. Jesus warns us that some will be surprised at their fate after this life because, although they may have done miracles in Jesus' name, He will declare that He never knew them (Matthew 7:23).

However, even genuine Christians make mistakes, and we have to admit that we don't always live up to our own standards, to say nothing about God's (Matthew 5:48; James 2:10). All of us need Christ's redeeming work in our life to transform us (Philippians 2:13). The reason our transformation is not automatic is that, although we've been saved from the *penalty of sin* (justification), we must choose at each moment whether we're going to resist the temptation to sin (1 Corinthians 10:13) and live according to God's plan for our lives. Every time we resist the temptation to sin, we are being saved more and more from the *power of sin* (sanctification). Ultimately, one day we will be released from these temptations when we are saved from the *presence of sin* (glorification).

So we need to remind our nonbelieving friends that Christians still can and do sin, even though we have been set free from the penalty of sin. God gives each of us a choice as to how we want to live our life and does not force us to submit to His will. God desires from us voluntary submission rather than forced compulsion.

Concluding Thoughts

Sour notes exist in non-Christian belief systems, and these must be surfaced and shown for what they are. Learning how to do this is a key part of Conversational Evangelism. It is often more helpful to allow a person to surface the truth for themselves rather than for us to identify discrepancies directly. In order to do this, we must discover the kinds of questions that can surface the uncertainty in the unbeliever's perspectives. This will often provide an opening for us to talk about Christ.

This requires us to improve our listening skills in conversations with others. Unfortunately, we do not always hear what people are saying, which creates difficulty in determining what they actually believe.

The result is that we may not have the right information to ask the kind of penetrating questions that will prompt interest in what we have to say. Instead, we may end up asking questions that do not surface the core issues but rather cause defensiveness and cut off any future dialogue.

The successful pre-evangelist must play the role of the musician— listening carefully for sour notes that non-Christian belief systems inevitably generate. Yet he must do more than listen to sour notes; he must really hear where people are coming from and understand more clearly their perspective in order to engage them in meaningful dialogue.

Reflection

1. Why do you think it's so hard for us as Christians to really hear what our nonbelieving friends are saying to us about their beliefs and values?

2. Is it your normal practice in a conversation of a religious nature to listen intently and patiently, especially with people you radically disagree with, in order to really understand what they are saying? Or do you tend not to listen so carefully because you're formulating a response in your mind to dismantle their argument?

3. How do we establish a better track record for hearing not just what we want to hear in our conversations with our non-Christian friends? What positive steps can we take to ensure we are being more objective in our observations?

4. How often do you think you have correctly anticipated what another person would say about his morals, values, or beliefs and answered accordingly?

5. What might be some negative results from pointing out right away what you believe to be problems with someone's statements?

Application

1. It is a common habit for people to interrupt one another during a conversation. Develop the habit of *patiently waiting* for the other person to finish speaking before taking your turn. This week I will practice the art of actively listening and try not to interrupt others as they are talking.

2. This week, during your conversations with your friends, practice making your response *relevant* to what the other person just stated. Also when witnessing to your non-Christian friends, practice listening for the *key words or phrases* the other person uses to determine your reply.

3. Poor listening habits or simple misunderstandings often lead to disagreements and hurt feelings. Practice thinking about whether you *fully understand* what other people say during conversation. If not, either *ask for clarification* or state what you think the person said and ask if you understood correctly. It's especially important to allow those who are willing to share more about what they believe to do so without too much interruption.

4. When you hear a person state what you think is one of the key components of their belief/value system, try to think if anything they said previously brings this belief into question. This may help you to help them surface the *discrepancies* in their own thinking and may invite more honest and open reflection and dialogue.

5. Practice identifying the different kinds of sour notes listed in appendix 3 (this exercise will help you identify these sour notes more quickly in conversations with others).

6. Record in appendix 1 what you are hearing from those on your top three list. Determine which of those issues could be the focus of a future conversation. At this point you

should not be concerned about what you are going to say; just determine what might be a good topic for conversation that could help them take a step closer to Christ.

7. Remember not to listen just to the labels people use to identify their religious beliefs. Listen intently to the words they use to determine what they *really believe* and whether they are mixing different worldview perspectives.

Chapter 4

Learning the Role of the Artist

Illuminate the Discrepancies

Interviewer: Do you think the Bible is reliable and accurate?

Student: Yes, I think it is reliable and accurate.

Interviewer: Why would you say that?

Student: Um, just going to church and…actually one of my youth ministers took it upon himself to try to prove the Bible wrong, just to see if he could. And every source that he found that could even come close to proving the Bible wrong, he found something even more accurate that countered what he was finding.

Interviewer: And so that convinced you that it must be true?

Student: Yes.

Interviewer: Do you know what the Bible says about who Jesus was?

Student: No, I don't.

Interviewer: The Bible says in John 14:6, Acts 4:12, and 1 Timothy 2:5 that Jesus is the only bridge or the only way to God. Did you know that?

Student: No, I didn't.

Interviewer: So is it possible to believe the Bible is reliable and yet not believe that Jesus is the only way to God?

Student: Um, I believe it's a matter of personal opinion. I don't think Jesus is the only way to God. I think there are other ways. That's my own personal faith. That's the conclusion I've come to, but I don't know how. But I think there are other ways to God besides Jesus.

Interviewer: So then the Bible is not completely reliable.

Student: No, I think the Bible is reliable. It's just a matter of whether I choose to follow the Bible or not.

Interviewer: Okay, but if the Bible is reliable and records what the apostles said, and the apostles said that Jesus claimed to be the only way, then either they were wrong or Jesus is right.

Student: I think uh…Jesus is right. I'm probably wrong.

The Need to Create Interest in the Gospel

In the world we live in, it's not enough for us just to proclaim the Gospel to those around us; we need to create an interest in it as well. Furthermore, for us to suggest that man's ultimate problem of sin can be taken care of only by faith in Christ sounds narrow, arrogant, and intolerant to many. Consequently, there is greater need today to change our sharing style to a more conversational approach and allow others to surface the truth for themselves rather than have it imposed on them. That's why questions are so helpful.

Learning the Art of Painting a Picture

The first step of the Conversational Evangelism model is that, like a *musician*, we want to *listen and hear what others actually believe*. Then and only then can we begin to hear the sour notes people are singing to us. The second step is that, like an artist, we want to paint a picture by using questions to help people see more clearly what they say they believe. As an artist, we need to paint a *mental picture* for those we witness to by asking probing questions that help them to see themselves in a truer light. We want them to see what we see without directly telling them what they should believe. Yet this image of themselves may be distorted. So by asking probing questions, we help fill in the details they are missing about themselves.

We want to ask our nonbelieving friends questions in such a way that they begin to see that something is not quite right about what they believe, and the truth is surfaced. By allowing them to surface the truth for themselves, we are leading them on a journey of self-discovery. We can do this by asking two kinds of questions.

First, we can ask them questions that clarify the meaning of *unclear terms*. Second, we can ask questions that *surface uncertainty or expose false beliefs*. Let's look more closely at what's involved in each kind of question.

Asking Clarifying Questions

The best way to ask clarifying questions is to ask "What do you mean by..."[1] Often people do not have the same understanding of key terms, and this question helps to clarify the meaning of those terms. For example, if someone says, "I'm a pretty good person so I'm going to get into heaven," we should ask, "What do you mean by 'good'?" If someone says, "Jesus is my Savior," we should ask, "What do you mean by 'savior'?" If someone says, "I believe that Jesus is God," we should ask, "What do you mean by 'Jesus is God'?" (In the East some people accept multiple gods, including Jesus, just to cover their bases and not offend any god.)

Clarifying Questions Help to Clarify Beliefs

Clarifying terms is especially important when witnessing to those who use common religious terms but not in the same way orthodox Christians use them. For example, Jehovah's Witnesses say, "We believe in Jesus Christ, who is the Son of God," but their use of "the Son of God" means something different than what orthodox Christians mean by the title. Jehovah's Witnesses believe Jesus is Michael the archangel, a created being. Likewise, Mormons say they believe in Jesus, but the Jesus they believe in is not the one revealed in the Gospels but a spirit being who was the brother of Lucifer.

Clarifying terms is also important when witnessing to our scientifically minded skeptical friends. For example, Intelligent Design (ID) proponent Phillip Johnson points out that some Darwinists equivocate in their use of the word *evolution*. Most naturalistic Darwinists do not take our position seriously and ridicule us for not believing in evolution. Yet what escapes their notice is that they are equivocating on what they mean by evolution. We believe there is evidence from nature that microevolution occurs (finch beaks that change length and bugs that develop resistance to certain pesticides).[2] It is macroevolution (from the goo to you) that we see no evidence for.

Another term that would be helpful to clarify with a naturalistic Darwinist is *evidence*. Both sides in the debate have different standards for what constitutes evidence. A naturalistic Darwinist does not believe it is necessary to sketch out a complete explanation for Darwinian pathways. Rather he believes he needs to show only that a pathway is *theoretically possible* (or conceivable).[3] On the other hand, an ID advocate insists that anything less than an explanation of how such pathways can become a reality is inadequate because he sees the high degree of complexity around him and is open to more than naturalistic explanations.

Further, Darwinists equivocate on the term *science*, affirming that the creationist view of origins is not science in the empirical sense of observable and repeatable events in the present. But in that sense neither is macroevolution based on science. They forget that both creationism and macroevolution are attempts to explain origins where the past event was not observed and cannot be repeated. Rather, we can get at it only indirectly through the principles of causality (every event has a cause) and analogy or uniformity (events in the past were like those in the present). If it takes an intelligent cause in the present to explain the complexity in a human language, for example, then we can reasonably posit an intelligent cause to explain the complexity in the first living cell.[4]

Clarifying terminology can play an important part in facilitating a meaningful discussion and clear up some of the confusion on both sides of an issue. Therefore, it is essential in our discussions with our pre-believing friends that we ask for clarification of terms, even if we think we know how they are using a certain word.

Clarifying Questions Help to Uncover the Nature of a Barrier

The practice of asking clarifying questions can especially be helpful in knowing how to uncover the nature of a person's spiritual condition. For example, a few years ago at Texas Tech University a student said he believed that Jesus was "the Son of God and that He died for us." At first it sounded as if he were a Christian, but when he was asked the clarifying question, "So what do you mean by 'died for us'?" his answer was surprising. He said Jesus died as a moral example to show us how we should live. While it is certainly true that Jesus was an example for us, He was more than just an example. He died in our place and for our benefit (Romans 5:8; 2 Corinthians 5:21). Yet had the clarifying question not been asked, we might have missed that this student was probably not a believer.

Clarifying Questions Help to Create More Honesty in a Discussion

Asking clarifying questions can also help the people we are speaking with be more honest with themselves and with us about what they really believe. This is an important benefit in our witness to others. For example, I once asked a taxi driver in the East what his religious beliefs were. At first he said he was a Buddhist. But when I asked, "What do you mean by 'Buddhist'? Are you a devout Buddhist?" he replied, "Well, I'm really a free thinker." His admission then led to a more honest discussion about his barriers to religious beliefs in general and to Christianity in particular.

Clarifying Questions Help to Create More Openness to Spiritual Dialogue

Asking clarifying questions may create an open door for more interactive spiritual dialogue or direct evangelism. On another occasion a taxi driver said straightaway that he was a free thinker, and I asked him, "What do you mean by 'free thinker'?" To my surprise, that simple question led to a spiritual dialogue in which I had an opportunity to share the Gospel with him.

Clarifying Questions Help to Minimize Unnecessary Defensiveness

Another benefit of asking clarifying questions about a person's beliefs is that it creates the greatest possible opportunity for spiritual dialogue without making a person unnecessarily defensive. If people perceive that our goal is to have them help us better understand their beliefs rather than to just prove they are wrong, they are more likely to have a more positive response to our probing questions. We are actually taking advantage of our ignorance about what that person believes so that we may be assured of receiving the least defensive response possible.

Clarifying Questions Help to Reverse the Burden of Proof

Clarifying terms is also helpful because it reverses the burden of proof from us to the person we are talking to. We call this the boomerang principle. When someone throws a tough question or accusation at you, instead of answering the question right away, turn that question around and place the onus on them.

For example, when someone says to you, "I think that Christianity is just a crutch," you can turn the question around and ask, "What do you mean by crutch?" If someone says, "I don't think the New Testament documents are a reliable record of what Jesus said and did," you can ask, "What do you mean by reliable?" You could further ask,

"Why are the New Testament documents not as reliable as some of the documents written around the same general time period, such as Josephus or Plato? If we believe Plato wrote accurately, why can't we know that the things the New Testament says concerning Jesus' life are also true?"[5] We are not trying to prove here that everything in the New Testament that is taught as true is true, though we believe it is. We are specifically asking why we can't know that some of the basic events of Jesus' life are true.

So when people raise questions and try to put us on the defensive, we can avoid falling into their trap by using the boomerang principle, which can merely be asking them questions about the terms they are using in their emotionally charged questions or statements.

This boomerang principle is not a novel idea. Jesus frequently used a similar approach, as in this exchange with the religious leaders:

> One day as he was teaching the people in the temple courts and preaching the gospel, the chief priests and the teachers of the law, together with the elders, came up to him. "Tell us by what authority you are doing these things," they said. "Who gave you this authority?"
>
> He replied, "I will also ask you a question. Tell me, John's baptism—was it from heaven, or from men?"
>
> They discussed it among themselves and said, "If we say, 'From heaven,' he will ask, 'Why didn't you believe him?' But if we say, 'From men,' all the people will stone us, because they are persuaded that John was a prophet."
>
> So they answered, "We don't know where it was from."
>
> Jesus said, "Neither will I tell you by what authority I am doing these things" (Luke 20:1-8).

Because asking a clarifying question is so different from the practices we normally associate with evangelism, it may not be easy for us to break old habits and use this approach. One helpful strategy to increase the likelihood that we do is to practice first with our Christian friends. Once we become accustomed to doing this, we may find it easier to engage our nonbelieving friends in a similar manner.

Asking Questions That Surface Uncertainty and Expose False Beliefs

In addition to asking questions that clarify the meaning of unclear terms, we also need to ask questions that *surface uncertainty and expose false beliefs*. Our goal here is to ask questions to help others begin to see the cracks in the foundation of their worldview. Ultimately, we want them to question whether their beliefs have a strong enough foundation to build their lives on. Seldom do people abandon their belief system unless they can see a better place to land.

This step can be broken into two different stages. The first stage focuses on asking our friends thought-provoking questions that *surface some uncertainty in their beliefs*. Even though this may not really challenge them to *change* their viewpoint, this can create some doubt that, over time, will expose the crack in their foundation, which may lead them to reconsider other aspects of their beliefs.

Exposing false beliefs usually doesn't happen overnight; it takes time. But just as a crack in a building's foundation may not do serious harm today but over time can lead to serious structural problems, a crack in our non-believing friend's worldview foundation today may result in changes later.

A good example of this is the conversion of Anthony Flew from atheism to deism because of the evidence for design. This didn't happen overnight. It took many years for the weight of evidence inherent in intelligent design arguments to inform his thinking. A small seed of doubt about the scientific evidence for atheism grew and over time led him to reject naturalistic explanations as fully adequate to explain the design in the universe. Likewise, our thoughtful and carefully worded questions could have an impact on our friends today that will bear fruit tomorrow.

Examples of the kinds of questions you may use to surface uncertainty are:

- "Do you think it matters what we believe, or is it more important that we have some kind of religion to make us a better person?"

- "Do you think that all religious beliefs basically teach the same thing?"
- "Do you think life has a purpose?"
- "Do you think human lives are valuable?"
- "Do you believe that some things are either right or wrong?"
- "Do you think that all people will be held accountable for the way they live? If so, what do you think the standard will be?"
- "Do you think the Bible gives us a reliable picture of what Jesus said or did?"

The second step then picks up where the first left off. Once our friends admit to some uncertainty in their beliefs, we can build on that by asking them more probing questions that *expose in a deeper way their false beliefs*. At the very least, we may create a greater doubt about their beliefs.

These follow-up questions may not even occur in the same conversation as your initial questions. They could, but it depends on the openness of the person you are engaged with in spiritual dialogue. Your follow-up questions could be asked a day later, a week later, or even a month or more later, depending on the prompting of the Holy Spirit and the person's openness to finding answers. As your questions surface more and more doubts, the person may be more open to further dialogue. That is one good reason why evangelism today must be an ongoing process (1 Corinthians 3:6).

Examples of follow-up questions are:

- "How is it possible for all religions to be the same when some of them contradict each other's key beliefs?"
- "How do you fit Jesus into your religious beliefs?"
- "How is it possible for there to be meaning and purpose in our lives and at the same time believe there is no God?"
- "How is it possible for human life to be valuable yet believe that life is just a random by-product of nature?"

- "How is it possible to believe that there is no God and yet believe in such nonmaterial things as truth and love?"

- "How can you claim there are absolutely no absolutes?"

- "How is it possible for us to empty ourselves from all desires?"

- "How can you say the Bible is unreliable when other ancient historical documents are accepted?" (An important question to ask our friends who are skeptical about the historicity of the New Testament and Jesus' claims to be the Messiah.)

- "Why do you think atheistic scientists insist that it is reasonable to believe that the natural world and the universe are caused by unintelligent causes when they exhibit features which in any other circumstances we would attribute to an intelligent cause?" (A question to ask those influenced by naturalistic Darwinism.)

  For example, would anyone really have any doubt that the presidents' faces carved on Mount Rushmore could be accomplished only by an intelligent cause? (Notice that we are not concerned here with whether the cause is supernatural or not, only that it is intelligent.)

- "If you were coming to the end of your life and you met Jesus and other great religious leaders and each suggested a different path, whose advice would you take? Wouldn't you take the advice of the person who has been to the other side and back?" (A helpful question to get people to think more about the uniqueness of Jesus.)

- "How can one know if the god they are worshipping is the right one?" or "How can you know if the gods you are not worshipping won't get jealous and cause trouble for you because of those you are worshipping?" (A couple of practical questions that are helpful for some in the East who embrace animistic beliefs.)

- "Why should you or I fear the lesser spirits rather than our creator who created both of us?" (Another helpful question for those reluctant to change their religious practices because of their fear of evil spirits.)

The Critical Need to Expose Cracks in Foundational Beliefs

If we fail to expose the faulty foundation of others' beliefs, many may not have any motivation to consider the person of Christ and His demands on their life.

Many college students in the West believe they will get to heaven by doing good works. They base that on their belief that they are mostly good, perform more good deeds than bad, have high standards, follow the Ten Commandments, treat others well, try their best, are humble, or are sorry for the bad things they do.[6] The key question that helps surface this false belief is, "Do you think Hitler will be in heaven?" Most would say they do not believe that Hitler will be in heaven. Yet, if they do not believe that Hitler will be in heaven, they have just admitted that there is a standard that Hitler falls short of but that other people measure up to. The follow-up question to them is, "What then is that standard that Hitler does not measure up to but that other people do?"

The Bible teaches us in Matthew 5:48 that the standard is perfection, and we are all aware that none of us can truly measure up to God's standard perfectly (see also James 2:10). Yet without exposing the faulty foundation they are resting on, many may consider their approach adequate to get them into heaven. So the right questions can help others to better face the truth.

Ray Comfort's "The Way of the Master" evangelistic material is helpful on this point.[7] The "good person test" based on the Ten Commandments is helpful for many from Western religious backgrounds. Most people who say they believe in the Ten Commandments can name only three or four of them.[8] And when asked whether they have ever lied, cursed, or lusted in their heart, they have to admit they have fallen short of the standard they say they accept. A couple of follow-up questions that are helpful here are:

- "Do you always live up to your own ideal?"

- "Do you always do to others what you want them to do to you?"

We all fall far short of the standards we've set for ourselves.

Using the Conversational Evangelism Approach with an Atheist

In talking with someone who professes to be an atheist or skeptic, a good penetrating question is, "If you could know the truth about religious issues (and at this point I'm not saying you could), would you want to know it?" After I asked a college student this question one day, he paused for several moments to think and finally said, "Yes, I would like to know it."

For those you sense may be resistant to coming to any conclusions about religious matters, you can follow up with this statement: "The reason I ask you this question is because the truth may have consequences you may not want to hear."

You can ask those hard-core professed atheists who you run into every so often, "Are you absolutely certain there is no God?" If they say yes, ask them, "Are you telling me that there is absolutely no God? How can you know this if there is no absolute truth? And if you do not have absolute truth, then is it not possible that there is a God?"

If they admit this, then they have gone from atheism to agnosticism. A good follow-up question here is, "If you could be shown some evidence that there is a God, would you be open to exploring further the claims of Christ?" If not, then further conversation might not be very helpful since they have demonstrated an unwillingness to search for the truth.

Using the Conversational Evangelism Approach with a Muslim

In talking with Muslims, a good penetrating question is, "Do you believe what the Qur'an says?" They will certainly answer yes. Then ask, "How do you resolve this dilemma? Does not the Qur'an itself consider the previous revelations contained in 'the book' to be authoritative and authentic revelations from God (Sura 2:136; 4:163)? And doesn't the Qur'an also state that 'None can change His word' (Sura 6:115;

see also 6:34; 10:64)? Then when, where, and how did the Bible get corrupted?"

You can also ask them,

- "If the Bible was preserved from the time of Jesus to Muhammad,[9] and the manuscripts we rely on today to translate our Bible are older than Muhammad,[10] when could the Bible have actually been corrupted?"
- "How come we cannot trust the Bible when it says that Jesus claimed to be God (John 10:30)?"
- "How come the Bible gives us so many examples in the New Testament where Jesus accepted worship from others?"[11]

If they continue to insist that all these Scripture passages have been corrupted, ask,

- "How can we determine then which parts of the Bible should be believed and which parts cannot be believed?"
- "If Jesus told the people of His day to check the Bible to see whether He was telling the truth, then would you believe what He said if I could show you that the New Testament today has the same message about Jesus (e.g., that He is the Son of God) as the one in Jesus' day?"

If they agree, then introduce them to a good book on this topic, such as F.F. Bruce, *The New Testament Documents: Are They Reliable?*, Craig Blomberg, *The Historical Reliability of the Gospels,* or Gary Habermas, *The Historical Jesus.* In brief, there are more Gospel manuscripts, earlier manuscripts, better copied manuscripts, written by more witnesses, with more historical and archaeological confirmation than for any other person or event from the ancient world. In light of this, a good question is: "If we can believe other people or events from the ancient world with much less evidence, then why should we not believe what the New Testament says about Jesus?"

Further, you can ask questions about what the Qur'an teaches about

Jesus because even the Muslims' own scriptures teach that Jesus was more than just a prophet (Sura Al-imran 3:42-55). You can also ask, "Do you know what makes Jesus unique? Did you know that even the Qur'an teaches that Jesus lived a sinless life (Sura 3:45-46; 19:19-21) and was virgin born (Sura 3:47)?"

We also know from secular and religious sources that Jesus did many miracles, such as walking on water, turning water into wine, and raising people from the dead. The Qur'an attributes no such miracles to Muhammad (cf. Sura 17:90-93).

Usually these kinds of questions are not going to change Muslims' views overnight, but they could help to reveal the cracks in their worldview foundation that over time the Spirit of God could use to draw them toward Christ or to be more open to consider His claims.

Using the Conversational Evangelism Approach with a Buddhist

In talking with a Buddhist, we can ask, "If desire is the source of all suffering, how do we desire to stop desiring?" Or, "Does it make more sense that we give up on the idea of desire or rather that we develop the right desire as Jesus taught (Matthew 5:6)?"

We can also ask Buddhists more practically minded questions such as, "If you were not sure if you should follow Jesus or other great religious leaders, consider this perspective. If you follow Jesus and you're wrong, you may have many other lifetimes to get it right. But if you follow other paths and you're wrong, you don't have any more chances to get it right (Hebrews 9:27). Wouldn't it be wise then to choose Christ first?"

Using the Conversational Evangelism Approach with a Hindu

Some key issues we can focus on when talking to Hindus are: the need for atonement, the reality of evil, the origin of karmic debt, and the problem with a plurality of gods. A deep hunger for a relationship with a personal God as opposed to the impersonal gods of Hinduism is another topic to pursue. These are all beliefs that we can ask our Hindu friends to clarify for us.

For example, in Hinduism the sin we have committed is that we have forgotten that in some sense we are God. Popular Hindu author Deepak Chopra says, "In reality, we are divinity in disguise, and the gods and goddesses in embryo that are contained within us seek to be fully materialized."[12] Yet we can ask our Hindu friends, "Does it make more sense that man's sin is that he has forgotten that he is in fact god, or is it more likely that man's sin is that he has fallen short of measuring up to the standards of a holy God?" We can further strengthen the point by adding, "especially when we all possess a moral compass and don't even measure up to our own standards of right and wrong?"

Conversational Evangelism in Action

Allow a personal example to show how we use these kinds of questions in the lives of the nonbelieving friends in our circle of influence. A few years ago our former nanny told us she was going to have to leave us for personal reasons. This made us very sad because not only was she a good nanny, but we had not had the opportunity to share the full Gospel with her.

So a few days before she left us, we asked her, "Aunty, how do you fit Jesus into your Buddhism?" In asking this question we were not encouraging her to add another god to her pantheon of gods she worshipped. We were asking her to consider how she was going to fit Jesus into whatever religious beliefs she had.

If she really understood the importance of fitting Jesus into her religious picture, then we could help her to understand that if we do accept Jesus into our lives, He demands exclusive worship. Yet the first step was to get her to realize that she should not exclude Jesus from consideration in forming her religious beliefs.

Apparently this thought-provoking question did make her think more deeply about her beliefs because after thinking about it for a few moments she said, "I haven't quite figured that out yet." That comment then gave us the open door to share how Jesus had made a difference in our lives. She did not make a decision that day to accept Christ, but we could tell by her reaction that our question had caused her to think more deeply about how inadequate her foundation for belief in Buddhism really was.

Asking a Probing Question Can Lead to a Crisis in Belief

When you and I paint a picture using questions that help others see that their foundation may not be strong enough to build their lives upon, this could lead to a crisis in belief. Certainly this occurred in the ministry of the apostle Paul when he challenged the beliefs of the polytheists in Athens.[13] As a result of Paul's dialogue, many of them were forced to consider the inadequacy of their beliefs, and this was instrumental in some wanting to continue the dialogue. For others it actually contributed to their putting their faith in Christ (Act 17:32-33).

The psalmist put the polytheistic dilemma in vivid focus when he said:

> But their idols are silver and gold,
>   made by the hands of men.
> They have mouths, but cannot speak,
>   eyes, but they cannot see;
> they have ears, but cannot hear,
>   noses, but they cannot smell;
> they have hands, but cannot feel,
>   feet, but they cannot walk;
>   nor can they utter a sound with their throats.
> Those who make them will be like them,
>   and so will all who trust in them.
>   (Psalm 115:4-8)

In short, how can we trust deaf, dumb, and blind idols we have made with our own hands?

The Importance of Being Selective in Using Questions

Many questions can be asked, but if we are going to effectively engage others in spiritual dialogue and even challenge them to reconsider their beliefs, we are going to have to learn the fine art of conversation. We must learn to engage others and ask questions that surface uncertainty and expose false beliefs and perspectives. Yet we must remember to be selective in what we talk about and the kinds of questions we raise.

It is easy for others to be turned off by our approach if they think we are operating like a slick salesperson and just trying to argue our case. It's also easy to turn others off from continuing their spiritual dialogue if they believe we are "piling on" and criticizing them. That is why it's so important to ask God for wisdom (James 1:5) about what issues or questions we should focus on. We need to discover that one issue that may open the door to help our friends uncover their real barriers to Christ or that would at least cause them to dig below the surface.

Asking Questions with the Three Ds in Mind: Doubt, Defensiveness, and Desire

In order to gauge whether we are asking the right questions in the right way to have maximum impact, another useful strategy is to keep three objectives in mind. We call them "The Three Ds of Asking Questions"— Doubt, Defensiveness, and Desire.

Many times we may ask questions in a way that produces unnecessary defensiveness, making it difficult for others to hear what we are saying and even leading them to cut off all future dialogue with us. Instead, we need to learn to ask questions in a way that *surfaces doubt* in nonbelievers' perspectives, while at the same time *minimizing their defensiveness* and *creating a desire* to want to hear more.

In doing so, we are following Jesus' example with the woman at the well in John 4. He did not tell her that she needed to turn from her sins or else she would burn in hell. He merely asked her thought-provoking questions and created in her a curiosity to hear more.

Mastering the three Ds of asking questions is especially important in today's world where people can be turned off quickly if they sense we are out to prove them wrong or make them look foolish. That's why it's so important that we learn not only what kinds of questions to ask, but also the best way to ask them.

I could ask someone, "Why would you want to believe something so stupid?" but this obviously does not encourage further conversation. Or I could ask, "Can you help me understand something that's confusing to me? You said A, but you also said B. How do you put these two things together in your own mind?"

To help us develop a Christ-centered perspective on how we use questions and to keep ourselves accountable in this area, we should ask ourselves the following:

1. Do we ask questions as one who is first and foremost interested in knowing, expressing, and living the truth as we dialogue with others with alternative perspectives?

2. Can we acknowledge to ourselves and even to others that we as believers do not have a handle on all the truth? After all, even the apostle Paul said in 1 Corinthians 13:12 that "now we see but a poor reflection as in a mirror," meaning that we don't see all of the truth all of the time.

3. Do we realize the importance of communicating truth (even what we have an absolute conviction about) in a humble and gracious manner (1 Peter 3:15) and with a teachable spirit.

If we want to be more effective in speaking to people in a way that we will be heard, we must remember these important steps.

The Importance of Doing More than Just Deconstructing Beliefs

We must also remember to do more than just deconstruct the beliefs of our non-Christian friends. When we ask probing questions, we must do so in a way that will make them more open and curious to hear more about our Jesus or at least continue the conversation at a later date.

Few people will get out of a leaky boat if they don't believe they can get into a better one. It would be better to plug up the hole or bail water. This is especially important in a postmodern world where there is an automatic rejection of anything that smacks of "absolute truth." Merely deconstructing someone's beliefs will have little shelf life in our witness to others unless we also develop in them an interest in either furthering the conversation or knowing more about our Jesus.

One day I was talking to a Chinese lady in an apartment. For several minutes she talked about how wonderful Buddhism was, so at an appropriate time I asked her, "But don't you as a parent desire good things for your children?" (In Buddhism you are supposed to get rid of all desires.) She realized that her actions didn't match her beliefs, and after a long pause she said to me, "Well, I've been a Buddhist for only a year. You should ask my mother."

Because I took the time to carefully and graciously reveal one crack in her belief about Buddhism, she was willing to hear what I would say next about Jesus.

"Do you know what Jesus taught about the problem of desire that Buddha was so concerned about?" I asked her. I then had the opportunity to explain that Jesus taught that the answer to man's problems was not to give up on desire but to develop the *right* desire. I further explained that Christians believe that when we invite Christ into our lives, He changes us from the inside out so that we no longer desire to do bad things, but we desire to do the good things God wants us to do (Philippians 2:13).

Summary

In the world we live in today, we need to allow others to surface the truth by asking them probing questions—questions that clarify the meaning of unclear terms and that surface uncertainty and expose false beliefs. Furthermore, to make sure our questions have maximum impact on those we are trying to reach, we need to remember the three Ds of Asking Questions (Doubt, Defensiveness, and Desire). We need to ask questions in a way that surfaces uncertainty while minimizing defensiveness and creating a curiosity to want to hear more. We also must be selective in the kinds of questions we ask our friends so as not to overwhelm them and make them unnecessarily defensive.

In a world that may not be so easily inclined to believe in any "good news" or to even think there is any such thing as "bad news," this combined strategy could be a helpful approach for clarifying beliefs, surfacing doubts, and creating more interest in our Jesus. This may play a role in helping our nonbelieving friends take one step closer to Christ (1 Corinthians 3:6).

Reflection

1. The process of painting a mental picture in the mind of the person concerning their belief system can come about only if we have taken the time to hear them clearly and understand their viewpoint. Having truly listened and clarified for yourself what the person you are talking to believes, you are then ready to ask questions that probe their own understanding of their beliefs. By this time, the person may be more inclined to entertain questions from you about what they believe and may be more open to some honest reflection and evaluation.

2. Remember that even though you think you may have a good understanding of what a person's beliefs are, it is still vitally important that you ask them clarifying questions about what they believe because misunderstandings can occur so easily. It is quite likely that they have not fully understood and reflected upon the entirety of what they say they believe. It's also possible you have not heard them clearly and may not know what questions would be most helpful to create spiritual dialogue and reflection.

3. Remember that a person may use terms and phrases as they talk about their belief system that sound similar to Christian terms, yet they may be using these terms in a different way. So be careful about making too many assumptions in your interaction with others. These assumptions could lead to a greater likelihood of miscommunication.

4. The truth of Christ is the foundation we build our lives upon. If you and I have committed our conversation to the power and guidance of the Holy Spirit, He will use our lives

and words to penetrate the minds and hearts of the people we are seeking to reach.

5. Train yourself to avoid the extreme of either glossing over or directly challenging discrepancies in what another person says. Rather, practice the fine art of asking questions in a way that helps the person to surface the truth for himself.

6. Remember that sometimes it is more helpful to answer a question with another question to give those who ask an opportunity to think more clearly about what they actually believe. Remember also that in normal dialogue we should resist the temptation to directly counter a challenge or even a difficult question because it could lead us to be defensive in our response, the very thing we want to avoid causing in them.

7. When you respond to your friend's questions in a non-defensive, reflective, and confident manner, it may also help your friend to listen more seriously to what you believe.

8. It is important that others see us as an ally who is trying to help them work through their struggles, rather than as an enemy they feel obligated to attack, even if they agree with some of what we're saying.

Application

1. Practice listening more intently in your conversations with others this week. You might be surprised how many questions for clarification come to your mind that may create opportunities for greater spiritual interaction. You also may learn to enjoy talking to people in deeper, more satisfying ways.

2. Consider also what terms you want those in your top three list to clarify for you that may create more open doors for spiritual dialogue. Record your insights in appendix 1 under step 2.

3. Reflect on the sour notes you have heard in the lives of your

top three and that you recorded in appendix 1 under "Hearing." Consider one key question that could create greater self-reflection or openness to discuss that sour note. Write down this question under step 2.

4. What one good follow-up question could you ask those on your top three list that builds on your key question? Record your answers in the spaces provided in appendix 1, step 2.

5. Consider one thought-provoking question that could create greater openness to continue the spiritual dialogue in future conversations. Record your answers again in appendix 1 under step 2.

6. What are some questions we can ask that keep in balance the three Ds of Asking Questions (Doubt, Defensiveness, Desire)? Record your answers in appendix 1, step 2.

Chapter 5

Learning the Role of the Archaeologist

Sam was very outgoing. After agreeing to let him help us save money on our phone bill, I began to ask questions about his life. Turns out he was a recovering alcoholic and had been sober for five years. He mentioned that he had to "give it over." I asked who he gave it over to, and he didn't name a specific person. He asked how our cell group meeting went the previous night. I asked if he went to church. He said he had been raised Catholic and it turned him off because of the hypocrisy and the judging of others. He shared briefly that he has friends who are gay.

I then used this analogy to try to uncover his real barriers to the Gospel. I asked him if he goes to restaurants. He said yes. I asked if he had ever had food poisoning from a restaurant. He again said yes. I asked if he ever went back to that restaurant again, and he said no. I asked if he goes to other restaurants. He said yes. I asked why he didn't stop going to all restaurants. Aren't they all the same? This huge smile came over his face, and he said he had never thought of it that way before.

I explained that churches are full of people, and we make mistakes. To not try other churches because of a bad experience at one was judging the others. He asked where he could find a good church. I told him about ours. I talked about purpose in life, and God wanting a relationship with us and having a plan for each of us. He told me he really appreciated me taking the time to *talk with him and to listen. I prayed for him. I hope this was the first step in getting him closer to Christ.*

Nancy

The Need for More than Deconstruction

The first step of the Conversational Evangelism model, the role of the *musician,* deals with the need to listen earnestly in order to understand our non-Christian friends' viewpoints. Then and only then can we learn to uncover the major sour notes in their beliefs. The second step, the role of the *artist,* focuses on asking probing questions that surface uncertainty about their beliefs while minimizing defensiveness and creating a curiosity to want to hear more. Now this third step, the role of the *archaeologist,* addresses helping others uncover the real barriers they have to embracing the Gospel.

Just as it's not enough for us to proclaim the Gospel to successfully reach people today, we must do more than just deconstruct someone's beliefs. We must be more than good listeners who know how to ask the right questions to help others see the potholes in their beliefs. A deconstructive approach alone is inadequate when emotional or spiritual barriers are keeping someone from even hearing what we're saying about Christ. The questions people raise about the Christian faith are often not the real barriers that keep them from trusting Christ. Jeremiah 17:9 says people's hearts are deceitful and wicked, which makes uncovering their hidden barriers difficult.

Furthermore, pre-evangelism must not be limited to surfacing discrepancies in others' beliefs. Postmodern people have lived comfortably with discrepancies in their beliefs for a long time and often prefer to live with distorted beliefs rather than change how they live. It may not matter what the evidence shows. Some may actually say, "It doesn't matter how much evidence you present to me for the truth of Christianity because I don't want to believe."

Therefore, it's important that we also learn to uncover the emotional and spiritual barriers that keep people from placing their faith in Christ.

Sometimes we need to go below the surface of people's stated concerns and speak to the real issues.

Going Below the Surface to Uncover Hidden Barriers

Like an archaeologist, we want to carefully dig into people's history to discover their real barriers and how they came to be on their current path. Dr. Gary Habermas has identified three kinds of doubt in his excellent book, *Dealing with Doubt.* People doubt for intellectual, emotional, or volitional reasons. Often on the surface their doubt seems intellectual. Only by digging deeper can we find out whether the doubt is emotional or volition. This is important, because apologetics deals with intellectual doubt for which there are intellectual answers. But if people don't want to believe for emotional or volitional reasons, then all the apologetics in the world is not going to convince them.

Sometimes the stated barriers are not the real barriers that keep others from taking a step toward Christ. Proverbs 20:5 says,

> The purposes of a man's heart are deep waters,
> but a man of understanding draws them out.

Consequently, effective pre-evangelism requires people with the foresight and wisdom necessary, not only to deal with people's stated questions or objections, but also to go below the surface and address their real barriers to faith.[1] We want to discern whether there are unspoken issues keeping a person from seriously considering a relationship with Christ. We want to explore what is getting in the way of honestly talking about God. In order to do this, we need to keep *at least seven steps* in mind as we ask God for wisdom to guide us in this process (James 1:5).

Determine Whether Questions are Legitimate or a Smoke Screen

The first step to uncovering hidden barriers is to determine whether their issue is a legitimate question or a smoke screen. Sometimes questions can be just a diversion to avoid the truth. To remove the smoke we need to ask questions such as, "If I could answer your questions in a way that makes sense to you, would that help you more seriously consider a belief in God and Christianity?"

If they answer no, we then know that their barriers are really not intellectual. Then, for clarity and greater awareness of their issues, we might say, "It seems as though your barriers are not intellectual but are emotional, spiritual, or some other kind of barrier. Am I right?" In asking this, you provide them an opportunity to come clean and tell you what is really getting in the way of trusting in Christ.

Sometimes in talking with a hardened skeptic a helpful question is, "If you could know the truth about religious issues (and at this point I'm not saying that you can), would you want to know it?" Another helpful question is, "What kind of evidence are you looking for that would help you resolve this issue in your own mind?"

Asking these kinds of questions will determine whether the barrier is legitimate, saving a lot of time in discussions with people who do not want to know the truth. For example, a former student mentioned that after talking to his friend and trying to build pre-evangelistic bridges to the Gospel, his friend finally said, "Even if you put all the evidence right in front of me, I still won't believe. I don't want to believe." This student realized his friend had been throwing up a smoke screen, and early in the conversation he should have tried to uncover the real barrier.

We could avoid hours of needless discussions with our friends who appear to be open to spiritual dialogue by asking questions that reveal the true nature of their objections. It could also provide the incentive for them to be more honest with us about what really is getting in the way of them considering Christ.

However, some people really don't want to know the truth. I was reminded of this one day when I had a conversation with a student who said, "It would be hard for me to change my worldview in favor of a belief in a theistic God because I would then have to admit that I was wrong in my thinking. I tend to be too arrogant to allow that to happen."

At least he was honest. Most people are not that transparent.

In attempting to discern whether a question or issue is legitimate or a smoke screen, you are helping your non-Christian friends not only to be honest with you, but more importantly to be more honest with themselves. This is an important step we need to help others take in their spiritual journey if we are to have any hope of seeing them take steps toward Christ.

Determine the Nature of Their Barrier

The second step to uncovering hidden barriers is to determine the nature of their barrier, whether it be intellectual, emotional, or a combination of both. Sometimes barriers can seem to be intellectual, yet once you dig below the surface by asking probing questions, you discover they are not. For example, if people ask a question about the problem of evil, we should not automatically assume their question is totally of an intellectual nature. Many who struggle with this question do so because of emotional issues. Perhaps someone they know suffered some kind of painful experience. So ask them, "Why is this question so important to you?" This exposes possible emotional issues that may be helpful to discuss. If we give an intellectual answer but the real issue is an emotional one, we may lose an opportunity to make real progress in someone's journey to the cross.

Michael Ruse, a philosophy professor and strong Darwinist advocate, spoke a few years back at a conference where some Intelligent Design leaders and Darwinist proponents were having an open dialogue. One of his stated problems with Intelligent Design was that he could not reconcile it with the problem of evil. We can only wonder whether he or a loved one suffered through some painful experiences that made it difficult for him to reconcile a belief in God with the problem of evil. Perhaps some emotional baggage issues were getting in the way of his seeing the truth of Intelligent Design and an Intelligent Designer. This may even be one reason why some of our naturalistic Darwinist friends may have such a strong aversion to anything supernatural. They may need to experience some emotional healing before they will hear the truth and its implications for their lives.

Here are some questions that could indicate the presence of emotional barriers:

- "How could a good God allow so much suffering and evil in the world?"
- "If God is real, how come there are so many hypocrites in the church?"
- "If God is there, why doesn't He answer my prayers?"

Other questions may indicate the presence of intellectual barriers such as:

- "It's been too long since Christ lived, so how can we really know what He said?"
- "How can there be absolute truth when so many people disagree on so many things?"
- "Since the Bible has been mistranslated so many times, how can we be sure what it originally said?"
- "It doesn't matter what you believe as long as it makes you a better person."
- "Since so many people disagree on so many things, there cannot be one right answer."

One way to handle tough intellectual questions is to learn how to reverse the burden of proof. For example, if someone questions the reliability of the Bible, you might ask, "Why would you reject the Bible when other books of antiquity are accepted without question?"

It's not easy to discern whether someone has an emotional barrier or an intellectual barrier or even a combination of the two. Discerning this is more of an art than a science, and requires much practice and a lot of wisdom from God. The bottom line is we must not speak to perceived intellectual barriers when the real problem is the emotional baggage weighing them down. We should deal with the perceived emotional barrier first because this will often help us determine how real their intellectual barriers are. This leads to the next important step.

Uncover the Specific Emotional Barrier

The third step to uncovering hidden barriers is to uncover whether they are carrying any specific emotional baggage. Once you've determined that the questions or issues are legitimate (not a smoke screen) and that their barriers are not primarily of an intellectual nature, then most likely you will discover serious emotional barriers in their path to the cross. Some people may carry so much emotional baggage that it makes it difficult for them to even understand the Gospel.

In a conversation I had with a college student, it was clear that little spiritual progress was being made. Something seemed to be blocking him from hearing what I had to say about Jesus. Finally, he confessed that the last Christian who talked to him had said, "AIDS is God's punishment for homosexuals." Well, that explained clearly why the message was not connecting with him. He could not hear what I was saying because he was emotionally hurt by this comment.

This is just one example of the emotional barriers that may hinder people from taking steps to Christ. Other barriers are negative childhood experiences or overbearing religious parents. The most common complaint voiced by nonbelievers is all the hypocrites in the church. After I spoke about the truth of Christianity on a college campus, an Asian student asked, "How come Christians seem nicer inside of church than outside of church?" This should be a sobering reminder that our nonbelieving friends are also listening for the sour notes in our lives. It should also motivate us to do whatever it takes to make sure that we are not an obstacle to our friends' taking steps toward Christ.

Uncovering emotional barriers is especially important in speaking with those in traditional cults. A good percentage of cult members join cults because of the emotional baggage they carry or because of their need to feel loved or a part of a community. If our goal is to tear down their arguments and expose their false beliefs, we may miss an opportunity to help them remove any barriers that may be hindering them from seeing the truth of Christ.

A while back my wife had a friend from a religious cult whose husband committed suicide. We took food over twice to let her know we cared about her as she dealt with her bitter grief. I found out later that not many from her fellowship came to visit her after her husband's death.

Ministering to people's emotional and spiritual needs must be first and foremost in our minds when we attempt to share the Gospel with them. They may have difficulty hearing what we have to say with our words about Christ, but they cannot escape what we say by our lives. We may be the only Bible some people ever read.

Because emotional barriers can be a real hindrance, we need to develop a strategy for dealing with this issue when we encounter it in our witness to others. Consider the following suggestions.

First, when we discover an emotional barrier in people, we should invite them to share their story with us. Second, show empathy and visible concern toward those who have gone through difficult emotional trials in their life. Third, affirm God's love and hope for them, either verbally or nonverbally. Let them know also that whatever difficulty they have suffered, God really does care for them and desires to know them personally (2 Peter 3:9). Fourth, if appropriate, apologize for how another brother or sister in Christ treated them. If another Christian said or did something that caused them pain, we need to acknowledge this wrong. This may also help them to see the reality of sin, which could help them consider why we need Christ in our lives. Fifth, tell them you will keep them and their situation in your prayers. In a postmodern culture, being a spiritual person is now more acceptable, so we should make the most of this important bridge. Sometimes telling people you will pray for them when they share a difficult struggle can play an important part in helping them to see Christianity in a truer light and open the door for future spiritual conversations.

Uncover Questions or Concerns Behind the Questions

The fourth step to uncovering hidden barriers is to determine whether an underlying issue is behind the questions or concerns people raise. It is essential to dig below the surface to uncover the real issues. Sometimes we can accomplish this by asking people to clarify why a particular question is important.

Jesus always seemed to know how to get to the heart of the matter in discussions with people. When a rich man asked Him, "Good teacher, what must I do to inherit eternal life?" Jesus asked, "Why do you call me good?" (Mark 10:17-18) to help him wrestle with who Jesus really was. When this man saw himself as living up to the requirements of the Law (v. 20), Jesus revealed to him where his loyalties really were (vv. 21-22).

When the Sadducees asked Jesus a hypothetical question about who in the resurrection would be the husband of a certain woman who had seven husbands, He got underneath their question and surfaced the true nature of their objection (Mark 12:18-27). He knew they didn't believe in the resurrection of the dead, so in referring to Exodus 3:6 in the Pentateuch, which they did believe in, He soundly refuted their belief that there is no resurrection.

Nonbelievers may say, "I think Christians are arrogant for claiming that Jesus is the only way to God." Yet behind this statement could be a more troubling perspective that we also need to deal with. The real issue may be that they think Christians believe they are better than others. Therefore, we must clarify that we do not mean to be prideful or prejudiced in making this statement; we're merely stating what we believe to be true about Jesus and help them understand that we are just one beggar telling another beggar where to find bread. For them to really grasp this truth, we must be careful that *our communication of this truth is coupled with a meek or humble attitude,* otherwise they may have difficulty hearing what we say.

Uncover Their Biggest Barrier

The fifth step to uncovering hidden barriers is to discover their biggest barrier to embracing Christianity. People raise all kinds of objections to Christianity. Yet they may not even verbalize to themselves the one thing that keeps them from putting their faith and trust in Christ. So when we ask questions that pinpoint the most important barrier, nonbelievers can search their hearts to discover what's really holding them back.

This can also help them to identify what doubts, if any, they may have about the Christian faith and determine if those doubts are intellectual, emotional, or simply a matter of their will.

So it is important that we continually ask the friends we're attempting to reach, "What is your biggest barrier out of all your barriers to Christianity?" We need to determine what is keeping them right now from putting their faith and trust in Christ.

One day a former student asked her seeking friend, "What is keeping you from making a decision to accept Christ right now?" The friend realized there was nothing keeping her from making that decision, and right there and then she prayed to receive Christ into her life. So in some cases we may discover that there aren't any obstacles standing in the way, and we simply need to invite our friends to take a step of faith and put their trust in Christ.

Yet sometimes people may raise intellectual barriers that they need answered. One student said, "It has been 2000 years since Jesus lived, so we can't really know what He did or said." Yet after I gave him an article on the evidence for the resurrection of Christ, this seemed to erase his intellectual doubts. Many have been helped by a good book on the resurrection, such as *The Resurrection of Jesus* by Dr. Gary Habermas. Removing intellectual barriers can play an important role in helping our friends to be honest with themselves and us about what's keeping them from putting their trust in Christ (Jeremiah 17:9).

For example, I talked to an Asian student about Christ over the period of about a year and answered some of his biggest intellectual barriers. One day he confessed he no longer had any intellectual objections that were keeping him from trusting Christ. His major remaining barrier was that he wanted to feel what it would be like to become a Christian before he made a decision to invite Christ into his life. On another occasion, an Asian student confessed, "One of my biggest barriers to belief in Christianity is that I am not brave enough to consider religious issues without taking into account what other people think." He may have been concerned about what his parents would think, which is a big barrier in the East.

So among all the barriers our friends have toward Christianity (whether they are intellectual, emotional, or spiritual barriers, or a combination of all three), our job is to uncover the biggest obstacle so that we can, over time, help them remove the obstacle and take a step closer to Christ.

Sometimes, however, the biggest barriers have nothing to do with the evidence but have more to do with lifestyle choices. A student who seemed resistant to spiritual dialogue said to me, "I know everything you are saying to me is true, but I just have some things in my life that I don't want to give up." I reminded this student of what martyred missionary Jim Elliot said: "He is no fool to give up what he cannot keep to gain what he cannot lose."

In the East two of the biggest barriers to embracing Christ are "family obligation or expectations" and "reluctance to give up certain ritual and religious practices for fear of consequences to one's own situation and family." To answer this latter concern we must demonstrate, as in the days of Elijah and the prophets of Baal, that we should fear and worship only Jehovah God and not the lesser persons or spirits (Luke 12:4-5).

Uncover Motivational Factors

The sixth step to uncovering barriers is to find out what would motivate nonbelievers to get answers to their questions about Christ. Some may be motivated by realizing how empty life really is without a belief in God. Discovering their motivation for exploring Christianity can be helpful as you continue to fan their spiritual interest. It could also give you greater insights about how to dialogue with them over time, and could suggest the most effective focus of your conversation.

One person told me, "My mother committed suicide three years ago, and I do not believe in God or Christianity. However, I realize if there is no God, there's ultimately no meaning or purpose to life, and I am not willing to accept that yet." Another person said his mother died a few years ago, and he believed that she was in heaven. His motivation in discussing spiritual matters was that he wanted to see his mom again.

So discovering the motivational factors can help remove potential obstacles and clear the way for us to build a bridge to the Gospel. It can also create a greater willingness on their part to dialogue with us long enough to help them discover what is really getting in the way of taking steps to the cross.

Uncover the Volitional Factor

The seventh and final step is to uncover the volitional factors. We want to attempt to surface an unwillingness to believe that goes beyond intellectual and emotional barriers. To some degree, everyone has a volitional problem with God's truth. Paul declared that all people know about God because He has made Himself known to them through His creation, and so people are "without excuse" (Romans 1:18-20). Yet they "suppress the truth by their wickedness" (1:18).

John bemoaned the Jews who had seen Jesus' miracles and yet refused His message: "Even after Jesus had done all these miraculous signs in their presence, they still would not believe in him" (John 12:37). Elsewhere, Jesus said of the hard-hearted, "'they will not be convinced even if someone rises from the dead'" (Luke 16:31). We can answer all their intellectual problems, uncover all their emotional barriers, and still some will refuse to believe.

So if we deal with all the barriers mentioned in points one to six and there remains an obstacle to faith, most likely the problem is of a volitional nature. Regardless of the evidence, they simply don't want to believe. Jesus said, "O Jerusalem, Jerusalem…how often I have longed to gather your children together, as a hen gathers her chicks under her wings, but *you were not willing!*" (Luke 13:34). To rephrase an adage: "You can lead a horse to water by pre-evangelism techniques, but only the Holy Spirit can persuade him to drink."

Here is where two great weapons in the Christian arsenal can be helpful: *love* and *prayer*.

God often uses prayer to reach the hearts of the seemingly unreachable. And it is our obligation to exercise it fervently (Luke 18) and effectively (James 5:16). It has been rightly said that "prayer is the slender nerve through which the muscles of omnipotence are exercised." And yet for our prayer to be effective, we must pray with the right posture. As one Christian writer says, "Until we are desperate that we have nothing, prayer is merely incidental, or at best, supplemental in our lives—but it will never be fundamental."[2]

Finally, since "God's kindness leads [us] toward repentance" (Romans 2:4), our final weapon against doubt and unbelief is love. Jesus said, "By this all men will know that you are my disciples, if you love one another" (John 13:35). Love is a more persuasive force than fear, and though many people are seemingly untouched by reason and argumentation, they are truly moved by our love for them. Jesus Himself confirmed that loving others was the second greatest commandment (Matthew 22:37-39). We shouldn't be surprised then that love can persuade the will to do what arguments alone are not able to convince the mind to do. By how we live our lives and love others, many may be attracted to learn more about our Jesus.

These seven factors can play an important role in helping us surface the real barriers that keep others from trusting Christ. We need to look continually for signs of unstated issues or concerns and help others discover what is really getting in the way of them putting their trust in Christ. While focusing on these issues alone may not lead to an immediate decision to accept Christ, they could play an important part in helping someone to take one step closer to Jesus (1 Corinthians 3:5-6).

Summary

As an *archaeologist* we want to *dig up nonbelievers' history to discover their real barriers to the Gospel and how they came to be on their current path.* In order to do this, we need to keep in mind the following seven steps as we ask God for wisdom to guide us (James 1:5). First, we must determine whether their issue is a legitimate question or a smoke screen. Second, we must determine the nature of the barrier, whether it be intellectual, emotional, or a combination of both. Third, we must uncover whether they are carrying any specific emotional baggage. Fourth, we must determine whether there is an underlying issue behind the questions or concerns people raise. Fifth, we must discover their biggest barrier to embracing Christianity. Sixth, we must find out what would motivate them to get answers to their questions about Christ. Seventh, we must discover whether the basic problem is an unwillingness to believe.

Once we uncover these barriers, we can then develop a strategy for moving our conversation from pre-evangelism toward direct evangelism. This is the focus of the next chapter.

Reflection

1. Remember that it's not easy to draw out someone's real objections to Christ. This may be true for most of us, and it is good to humbly admit this. We need to ask God for wisdom to know how to talk to people (James 1:5) about the things that bother them the most about Christianity.

2. Sometimes the real objections someone has to the Christian faith may be below the surface and may have nothing to do with their stated concerns. Therefore, we should pray that God would give us spiritual eyes to see what is really going on.

3. Sometimes people ask us questions about our Christian beliefs not because they are seekers of truth (they may not think that is even possible in our postmodern world), but because they either want to make us look foolish or they desire to make it harder for us to talk to them about Jesus. We need to always make sure their questions are legitimate before we attempt to answer them.

4. Our goal is not to pry into another person's deep personal issues. We want to invite the person to think about and to share his reasons for resisting Christ. If we do this carefully

and respectfully, he may be willing to reveal more about what troubles him about the Christian faith. We shouldn't try prying it out of him if he's not comfortable telling us.

5. No matter how clear you are in explaining the Gospel to your non-Christian friends, they may not understand if they are carrying around emotional baggage that keeps them from wanting to see clearly the truth about Christ.

6. Have you ever tried to share the Gospel with your friends and it seemed as though someone or something was blocking them from hearing what you were saying (see 2 Corinthians 4:4)? Think back on what kind of baggage they may have been struggling with that may have made it difficult for them to hear what you had to say about Jesus. Think about how you would handle the situation differently next time based on what you learned in this chapter.

7. The next time a person hits you with rapid-fire questions that challenge your faith in Christ, rather than trying to answer all of his questions, ask him which question is most troubling to him and why. If there are questions you don't have an answer for, admit this and commit to return with an answer. If you don't give the impression that you have all the answers, this may cause the person to be more open to what you have to say.

8. Remember that it's the Lord's responsibility to speak to the heart of the person we're attempting to reach. We are just His messenger, and He has given us the privilege to speak on His behalf.

Application

1. Ask your spouse or another good friend to play the role of the skeptic with you. Practice listening intently and responding with a patient, sincere heart as you encounter barriers.

2. Ask yourself which questions you could ask your "top three" non-Christian friends that could help uncover their

real barriers. Record your ideas in the space provided under step 3 in appendix 1.

3. List the different obstacles to the cross you have uncovered in your conversations with your "top three." Record your ideas in the space provided under step 3 in appendix 1.

4. Ask yourself what seems to be their major obstacle. Ask God for wisdom to help you discern what this could be. Record your answers in the space provided under step 3 in appendix 1.

Chapter 6

Learning the Role of the Builder

David: Can you help me understand something that is confusing to me about some Muslim practices in certain parts of the world?

Taxi driver (a professed Muslim): Sure.

David: Why is it that some radical Muslims think it's okay to blow up other Muslims caught in harm's way if they kill some "infidels" in the process? I can see how some could interpret the Qur'an to teach that it's okay to kill infidels, but how can they stretch the interpretation to include killing their cousins?

Taxi driver: I don't know. I think they are crazy.

David: But you know as well as I that this is not the belief of just a few isolated Muslims. Thousands and maybe even millions of Muslims believe this.

Taxi driver: I don't understand why they think this way.

David: Actually, I think I know one of the major reasons. Would you like to hear it?

Taxi driver: Sure!

David: It's partly because some radical Muslims teach that the only way they can have any assurance of getting to heaven is if they die in a holy jihad. As you know, even Muslim clerics don't have the assurance they're getting to heaven. Only those who die in a holy war. That's why so many radical Muslims are willing to commit suicide if they think it assures them a place in heaven.

Taxi driver: Well, I know there are some things that both Muslims and Christians do agree on.

David: That's true, but one key difference between Christianity and Islam is that as Christians we believe we can have an assurance of a relationship with our creator after this life is over. Unfortunately, this kind of assurance is not something Muslims can have if they follow strictly what Muhammad taught. Would you like to hear why I, as a Christian, can be assured that I'll go to heaven when I die?

Taxi driver: I am not sure that's possible, but yeah, go ahead.

The Role of Each Step in Conversational Evangelism

Now that we are at step four, the *builder,* we're ready to build a plan of action that could open the door to share the Gospel message with others. In step one, the *musician,* the focus was on listening and hearing "sour notes." In step two, the *artist,* the focus was on asking questions to clarify beliefs and surface uncertainty. In step three, the *archaeologist,* the focus was on uncovering nonbelievers' real barriers to faith. Step four then takes all that we've learned in the previous three steps and builds a plan of action.

As a builder, *we want to build a bridge to the Gospel,* and this building process involves at least six steps.

Overview of Building Conversations

First, we want to find the right balance in our approach between objective evidence and subjective experience (Acts 14:1; Philippians 1:14). Second, we need to find common ground with those we're trying to reach. Third, we also want to construct a bridge from a point of shared beliefs, though nonbelievers may not be aware of them. Fourth, we want to memorize a basic outline for defending the Christian faith. Fifth, we want to remember the goal (2 Timothy 4:2), which is to remove the obstacles so that we can help people take one step closer to Jesus (1 Corinthians 3:6). Sixth, we want to actively seek to build a positive case for Christ and look for opportunities to transition from pre-evangelism to evangelism.

Building a bridge to the Gospel is seldom easy, and this is especially difficult today because of the hostility toward those who claim to know the truth. Because of the erosion of truth, there is no longer a clear pathway for some to take steps toward the cross.

Let's examine these six steps in more detail.

Finding the Right Balance in Our Approach

First, we want to find the right balance in our approach between *objective evidence* and *subjective experience*. When we talk about giving *objective evidence* for the Christian faith, we're referring to evidence for such things as the resurrection of Christ (1 Corinthians 15:14) or the evidence from science that God exists. When we talk about *subjective experience*, we're referring to the evidence of God in our own lives demonstrated in how we live. Many were affected by the way the apostle Paul lived his life (Philippians 1:14).

In a postmodern world, both objective evidence and subjective experience are important to communicate in our witness to others. What may be difficult to decide at times is what kind of evidence will have the greatest impact on those we're trying to reach. Many people may care little about our objective evidence for the Christian faith until they see Christ in our lives and believe they can trust us. So a testimonial approach to witnessing can be fruitful in certain situations, especially with close friends or family members who know us well and may be attracted to what we say after they see our changed lives.

Yet there are also limitations to just letting others see Jesus in our life or sharing our personal testimony. Others may see that as just "our personal truth" but not "their truth." One person might say, "Because I've experienced Christ in my heart, I know the Bible is true." Another person might say, "Because I've received a burning in my bosom, I know the Book of Mormon is true."

How can our nonbelieving friends determine what is true if all we do is share our personal experience of Christ? We need to include along with our testimonies some of the objective evidence that shows the uniqueness of Christ. The apostle Paul said himself that "if Christ has not been raised, our preaching is useless and so is your faith" (1 Corinthians 15:14). So our faith can have validity only if it has an objective reference point.

Finding Common Ground

Second, we need to find common ground with those we're trying to reach. The apostle Paul said, "To the weak I became weak, to win the weak. I have become all things to all men so that by all possible means I might save some" (1 Corinthians 9:22). To find common ground means to find that point of intersection between our beliefs and those of our non-Christian friends. This is possible because of general revelation and common grace shared by all human beings (Romans 1:19-20; 2:12-15).

Let us illustrate what we mean by common ground. One day we had a conversation with a Jewish agnostic on a college campus. He mentioned how angry he was at all the Christians who tried to witness to him using the Bible when he did not believe that the Bible was reliable. He was not even certain that God existed. Our first step was to find common ground with him in talking about truth. Now to make a long story short, the last thing he said was, "You're going to have me up all night trying to figure this out." He responded differently to us because we sought to find that common ground before telling him about Christ. So, finding common ground involves discovering those mutually shared ideas that can be a springboard for deeper spiritual dialogue with our nonbelieving friends.

Finding common ground is especially important in a world that is more and more fragmented and has given up not only on the idea of absolute truth but also the correct use of reason. For example, for those who claim to hold a Christian perspective and yet depart from it in some major way, it is important in our dialogue that they embrace this truth: God's truth may go beyond reason, but it can never go against reason (2 Corinthians 1:18).

God never contradicts Himself in what He teaches us in the Bible. So although many humans were involved in writing the Bible, God is the ultimate author (2 Peter 1:21), and God cannot contradict Himself in what He teaches. Whatever Scripture teaches in one passage cannot contradict what is taught in another passage. Once we agree on this, it may make our discussion more fruitful because there is mutual agreement that whatever view we hold, that view cannot contradict other parts of Scripture.

In order to discover these areas of common ground, especially with those with little religious background, one helpful idea is to ask low-key questions such as,

- "Does it matter what you believe?"
- "Can everyone be right?"
- "Is just faith enough?"
- "Is there any difference between Jesus and other religious leaders?"

This certainly is not a novel idea. As mentioned before, Paul used different approaches depending on the audience he was speaking to. When he spoke to the Jews and the God-fearing Greeks (Acts 28:23), he used one approach, but when he spoke to the polytheists (Acts 17:22-31), he used another. He always sought to find common ground. In Acts 28 Paul merely showed that Jesus was the fulfillment of the Old Testament prophecies written about Him. Paul did that because his audience already accepted the idea of a monotheistic God. They also already accepted the authority of the Old Testament and had some ideas about the Messiah, though their picture of the Messiah was distorted. But in Acts 17, when speaking to polytheists who did not accept the Old Testament or a belief in a monotheistic God, Paul talked about the unknown God that they worshipped and used that point of connection to talk about the characteristics of the Christian God, who made the universe.

The Value of Positive Deconstruction (Finding Areas of Agreement and Disagreement).[1] One of the values of using a positive deconstructive approach is that we are always looking for areas of agreement with those we talk with, even if we disagree with most of what they say. For example, if someone says to us, "I believe that all religions are the same," we can say in response, "I agree with you that there are some similarities in all religions, such as the injunction to be good or kind to others." However, we should also say, "But while there are some similarities, there are also major differences. For example, each of the major religions has a different perspective about salvation."

Taking the time to build this common ground may help create more willingness on their part to dialogue about things they disagree with us on or at least have doubts about.

In a positive deconstructive approach it is also helpful first to "walk in their shoes." This is especially helpful in our witness with those from religious cults. Often we seek to expose the errors in the thinking of cult members without appreciating the difficulties in our own theology. As a result, we don't come across as the sincere seekers of the truth that Jesus encouraged us to be (John 8:32).

Before we critique someone's beliefs, we need to understand better what they actually believe and why. It can also be helpful for us to understand why they feel so strongly that we are wrong. We need to attempt to see life from their perspective. Perhaps by better understanding other people's concerns about our own beliefs, we can better communicate the truth of Christ in a way that will make sense to them.

Finding common ground is something we can do with almost anyone. As Christians we can even agree with atheist Richard Dawkins when he says that "God's existence or non-existence is a scientific fact about the universe, discoverable in principle if not in practice."[2] We can also agree with him when he says, "The fact that a question can be phrased in a grammatically correct English sentence doesn't make it meaningful, or entitle it to our serious attention."[3]

It is important then when we talk with others who have radically different views than our own to look for those areas we have enough in common so we can at least have an interactive dialogue.

Finding Common Ground Equals Earning the Right to Be Heard

Sometimes finding common ground can be merely earning the right to be heard. A former student related his experience in building common ground with a taxi driver.

> I went into this taxi where the driver was playing some Buddhist mantras over his sound system. He asked me politely if I minded and offered to turn it off if I did. Actually I did mind, but I decided to use the opportunity to ask him what he was playing. He told me what it was and asked if he could explain it to me. He also asked which religion I belonged to, which I answered Christianity. I agreed to hear his side provided he was open enough to hear my side at the end of his.
>
> He then began an exposition on his Buddhist faith that he enjoyed immensely, talking about how he tries to be as good a person as possible At the same time, he boasted how he was open to other faiths as well. So I asked him if I could share why I felt Christianity was different...By the time we reached my destination, I had taken the opportunity to invite him to my church (likewise, he had invited me to attend some of his Buddhist meetings)...
>
> I realized what made him open up to me initially was the fact that I was open to him to start with. Though he did not say it explicitly, I had to "hear" his desire to continue listening to his mantras, following which I bothered to "hear" about his faith. By allowing him that, the common ground of understanding was laid and he was open to listen to my view.[4]

Merely taking the time to hear what someone believes and genuinely showing interest in them may create the kind of common ground that will make it easier for us to pursue further spiritual dialogue.

Constructing a Bridge from a Point of Shared Beliefs

Third, once we find common ground with those we're trying to reach, the next step is to construct a bridge to the Gospel from those shared beliefs, building with planks of common understanding. These common understandings may be things that our nonbelieving friends are not aware of unless we help them to surface the truth by asking probing questions or unless some crisis in their world makes it more difficult for them to suppress the truth (Romans 1:18).

Furthermore, if they develop a new perspective on some issue that we did not share a mutual agreement on in the past, that new understanding can also be used as a foundation to build common understandings. For example, the events of 9/11 surfaced in many nonbelievers' eyes the importance of what one believes. Not all beliefs can be equally justified. In a pluralistic age this is an important plank to build on because so many today have bought into the idea that there are no major differences between religious beliefs. To admit, however, that the terrorists' religious beliefs were wrong implies a new perspective: not all views are the same or not all views can be right!

Science provides another example of how a new perspective can lead to other changed beliefs. Since Darwin published his *The Origin of Species,* scientists have learned many new things about our universe and the life around us that have called into question naturalistic explanations for its origins. For example, Darwin assumed that life at the cell level was not very complex. Now we know differently. For years many scientists even doubted that the universe had a beginning until some experiments in the 1990s pretty much disproved the steady state theory and gave strong support for the universe having a beginning.[5] This changed belief that the universe is not eternal led to another changed belief among some scientists that materialistic evolutionary theory is inadequate to explain life as we know it in such a short period of time.[6]

Once you agree to lay down one or more planks of common understanding, you may find it easier to lay down additional planks. If someone affirms the truth that "Not all views are equal" and "Not everyone can be right," then the question to ask is, "Would you agree then that some religious views must be wrong?" You may be surprised to find that this is the first time your nonbelieving friends have considered this as a possibility.[7] If they accept this also as a common plank, the next question you can ask is, "Then how do you decide who is right and who is wrong?"

At this point you have laid down enough planks in your bridge that it might create enough openness for you to talk about Christ and what makes Him unique.

Determining Whether a Heart or Head Bridge Would Be More Fruitful

These bridges can be either *head bridges* or *heart bridges*. Both are important in dealing with those affected by postmodern thinking. *Heart bridges* help people to understand how Jesus satisfies the very longings of their hearts and helps them to realize their hopes. True meaning in life can be found only in having a personal relationship with God. Christian apologist Ravi Zacharias says, "Jesus stated without a doubt that God is the author of life and that meaning in life is found in knowing Him."[8]

Building heart bridges. In building bridges with others, heart bridges generally are the most important to build first. To reach people in a world that has given up on reason and rationality, sometimes the Holy Spirit needs to break through their thick walls and penetrate their hearts. We need to be able to help people understand first and foremost how Jesus makes a difference. It is especially helpful to explain all those things that Jesus stood for that are attractive to a postmodern mind.

Recently I asked a Christian college worker with a Hindu background what was the turning point for him to come to faith in Christ. He said that the heart bridge that had the biggest impact on him were the words of Jesus on the cross, "Father, forgive them for they know not what they do." In an age that equates forced obedience with fundamentalist beliefs, this is an important heart bridge to remind our seeking friends that Jesus did not teach us to hate our enemies but to love our enemies and to pray for those who persecute us (Matthew 5:44). This is a refreshing truth about Christianity that can be an important heart bridge in our friends' journey to the cross.

Building head bridges. While constructing heart bridges may be our first step in reaching those affected by postmodern thinking, it cannot and should not be our only approach. Many today may claim they have no need for a savior since they have no sins to forgive. But even though they may not feel a need for Christ, that doesn't mean the need doesn't exist. We need to make the case that Jesus stands alone among religious leaders and challenge nonbelievers to rethink their pluralistic views.

To construct these important *head bridges* we need to use "planks of common understanding," as we talked about earlier. One of the most important head bridges to establish is the understanding that faith must have an object to be valid. Unfortunately, even many Christians don't clearly understand that *it is not faith that is important, but the object of our faith that is important.*[9] While we can take Buddha out of Buddhism and still have Buddhism, and we can take Muhammad out of Islam and still have Islam, we can't take Christ out of Christianity and still have Christianity. Specifically, we cannot take the resurrection out of Christianity and still have Christianity. The resurrection is foundational for the Christian faith (1 Corinthians 15:12-20).

Building Planks of Common Understanding

Here are some examples of planks we may use to build both head and heart bridges with those who are skeptics, pluralists, or postmodernists:

- "It matters what you believe because what you believe will affect how you live."
- "Not all religious viewpoints can be right."
- "Faith must have an object to have merit."
- "Jesus' claims are unique compared to any other religious leader" (John 10:30; 14:6; Acts 4:12; 1 Timothy 2:5).
- "The proof of Christ's claims have no parallel among major religious leaders."

- "Without God, some people find it difficult to find meaning in their life."

Under each point, you may want to ask your nonbelieving friends questions that help them to acknowledge the truth of each plank so that they surface the truth for themselves rather than having you tell them what they should believe.

The average college student will be reluctant to acknowledge that "if not everyone can be right about religious beliefs, someone must be wrong." Yet, we have found in our discussions with college students that once they are shown a simple chart describing different worldviews, many realize that someone has to be wrong. This inevitably leads us to ask them, "So then how do you decide who is right and who is wrong?" In many cases, this question may lead to an opportunity to talk about Christ.

Another helpful plank in building our bridge is the truth that the proof of Christ's claims have no parallel among any religious leader. For example, one helpful question we can ask our pluralistic-minded friends is, "Are you aware of the major differences between Christianity and all other major religions?" We can point out that Buddha claimed to point to the way, Muhammad claimed to be a prophet of God, but Jesus Christ is the only religious leader who ever claimed to be God, who lived a sinless life, who fulfilled prophecy written hundreds of years before He was born, and then died on the cross and rose from the dead. This helps them to begin to see just how unique Jesus really is.

Unfortunately, there is a tendency today to reduce the claims and evidence for the Christian faith to the same level as the claims for other religious beliefs. There is a tendency to say that comparing Christianity with other religions is like comparing apples with apples. This tendency was graphically illustrated a few years ago when I was chatting with a person on a plane. This man grew up in the church, but he said, "No one has ever given me any evidence for the Christian faith." So I explained to him just a little bit of the evidence for the resurrection of Jesus Christ. He interjected loudly, "But what about Buddha and what about

Muhammad?" I doubt that he raised this question because he thought Buddha and Muhammad had credentials like Christ's. More than likely it was because he was feeling the conviction of the Holy Spirit and was trying to level the playing field so that Christianity was no better than any other religion.

Our job in building bridges to our nonbelieving friends is to help them understand that Jesus truly is one of a kind.

If we are going to be successful in engaging others in pre-evangelism, it is important that we build specific kinds of bridges for certain kinds of people. For example, a useful tool in building bridges with a Muslim is the "Camel Method"[10] where "we can use the Koran to lift Jesus out of prophet status and closer to Savior status in the mind of a Muslim."[11]

With those who profess some form of Darwinist materialism, we can use these steps drawn both from science and philosophy:

- The evidence of an intelligent being can be inferred philosophically from principles of cause and effect and from design in nature.

- The evidence from astronomy favors a belief in the beginning of the universe.

- Even though one may try to explain the operation of the universe by purely naturalistic causes and processes, it still doesn't negate the need to explain the origin of the universe.

- Evolution may attempt to explain first life forms but not first life.

Conclusions: Evolution does not make belief in God unnecessary. Yet a belief in an intelligent creator does become necessary to explain the *origin* of life, whether natural processes in evolution can account for new life forms without some kind of intelligent intervention.

Memorizing the Overall Apologetic Outline

Apologetics is a systematic and rational defense of the Christian faith. By *systematic* we mean setting forth the logical steps one after the other.

(Elsewhere, we have identified twelve steps in presenting a logical and comprehensive approach to the defense of the Christian faith.) [12]

Now the fourth step in building a bridge to the Gospel is to memorize each step in the apologetic outline listed below. Memorizing the outline helps you know where to begin with the persons you are witnessing to. If they do not believe in truth, then you must begin at point one. If they believe all views are true, then point two is where to begin. If they believe in truth but not in God, then you can start at point three, and so on.

Knowing this argument in defense of Christianity will help you know where the person is and where to begin with them. A former student said,

> The main difficulty I had in applying the Conversational Evangelism approach was effectively linking one question or argument to the next to lead the person to a clear conclusion. I often felt somewhat muddled in the conversation. I realize I need to focus on understanding and remembering the logical progression of points so that I can help someone to see and understand them.

Understanding these twelve points will give you practical ideas on how to build effective *head bridges* to the Gospel. In logical order, the twelve points for establishing the case for Christianity are:[13]

1. Truth about reality is knowable.

2. The opposite of true is false.

3. It is true that a theistic God exists.

4. If God exists, then miracles are possible.

5. Miracles can be used to confirm a message from God.

6. The New Testament is historically reliable.

7. The New Testament says Jesus claimed to be God.

8. Jesus' claim to be God was miraculously confirmed by:

    a. He fulfilled numerous prophecies about Himself;

    b. He lived a sinless and miraculous life;

    c. He predicted and accomplished His resurrection.

  9. Therefore, Jesus is God.

  10. Whatever Jesus, who is God, teaches is true.

  11. Jesus taught that the Bible is the Word of God.

  12. Therefore, it is true that the Bible is the Word of God and anything opposed to it is false.

Don't Forget the Goal

Fifth, we need to remember not to get so caught up in pre-evangelism that we forget the goal, which is to remove the obstacles so that we can help people take one step closer to Jesus each day (1 Corinthians 3:6). The goal is to find opportunities to move from pre-evangelism to direct evangelism. If we deal only with pre-evangelistic issues and never get around to sharing the Gospel, we are not fulfilling God's mandate to be salt and light (Matthew 5:13-16).

Unfortunately, we can lose sight of our goal and become overly argumentative. We may win the battle but lose the war because of how we come across to others. We need to avoid falling into the trap of thinking that the important thing is to make sure that others know we are right.

At other times we fail to see the big picture so we don't even resolve to take the first step to build bridges to the cross in our daily conversations. Those who have a grasp of the importance of pre-evangelism and yet never engage others may not understand the lordship of Christ in their lives. They don't see, as the apostle Paul saw, that we have an obligation to help others take steps toward Christ (1 Corinthians 9:16-17). They get so involved in their daily affairs that they lose a kingdom mentality. We must make sure that training in pre-evangelism is reinforced with discipleship training.

If we keep sight of our goal and maintain a kingdom mentality, we will know that it's not important that we are able to twist the arm of nonbelievers so that they cry out "uncle" and agree with our beliefs; rather, we want others to see the truth about Christ so they will cry out *"Abba, Father"* (Romans 8:15).

Transitioning from Pre-evangelism to Direct Evangelism

Sixth, we should actively seek for opportunities to transition from pre-evangelism to direct evangelism and sharing the Gospel. Here we can integrate this pre-evangelism model into whatever method we are using to explain the Gospel. Sometimes when transitioning from pre-evangelism to evangelism, it is helpful to ask, "Has anyone ever explained to you the difference between Christianity and all other religions? I can explain the difference using just two words—*do* versus *done*."[14] This is a helpful approach because it likely will create some curiosity with those you are speaking to. They may wonder how you can explain the difference using only two words.

All the religions in the world, except for Christianity, say "do this" to get to heaven (or the equivalent). Muslims say, "Your good deeds have to outweigh your bad deeds." Hindus say, "You have to overcome karma and reincarnations by doing good works." Buddhists say, "You need to get rid of desire through an eight-fold path." All the religions of the world say you have to do something.

Christianity, on the other hand, is not about doing something but about what has already been done. The Bible teaches us that there is nothing we can do to earn a relationship with God. No matter how good I am or what I do for God, it will never be enough to earn the right to have a relationship with Him (Ephesians 2:8-9; Titus 3:5). That is why the focus in Christianity is not on *do* but *done*. Jesus provided the sacrifice to atone for my sins (Romans 5:8). My responsibility is to accept what God has *done* for me and allow Christ to come into my life (John 1:12) and change me from the inside out—not in my own power, but in His strength (Philippians 2:13; 4:13).

If the analogy of "Do versus Done" causes your nonbelieving friends to be open to talk about Christ, you can then offer them a more detailed explanation of the Gospel, whether you use a Bible or maybe a tract you're familiar with. Your pre-evangelism becomes seamlessly and effectively woven into your evangelism and witnessing style.

In order to build a bridge to the Gospel, it is helpful to keep these *six steps* in mind:

- find the right balance in your approach
- find common ground
- construct a bridge
- memorize an outline
- remember the goal
- actively seek to transition from pre-evangelism to direct evangelism

By utilizing these six steps over time, you may find your non-Christian friends making real progress in their spiritual journey to the cross.

Conversational Evangelism in a Nutshell

In brief, Conversational Evangelism involves listening carefully to others and *hearing* the discrepancies in their views and then *illuminating* those discrepancies by asking questions to help clarify their religious terminology and *expose* the weaknesses of their perspective. Then, we want to dig up their history and uncover their underlying barriers to *build* a bridge to the Gospel (1 Corinthians 3:6).

We must always begin with *hearing* conversations. Yet knowing what to do next is more of an art than a science. We may want to ask *illuminating* questions about the discrepancies we hear or we may next want to dig up their history a little to find out how they came to be on their current path before we ask any questions that help them to surface the truth for themselves. Each situation is different, and one approach may not work as well as another. We need to be sensitive to the Holy Spirit's leading (James 1:5).

The most important thing is that pre-evangelism should involve at least four different aspects: hearing, illuminating, uncovering, and building. These correspond to four kinds of roles that we can play in the life of our nonbelieving friends: musician, artist, archaeologist, and builder. Understanding how to integrate these aspects of pre-evangelism into our evangelism training can play an important part in helping us to more effectively reach the skeptics, pluralists, and postmodernists of our day.

May God help us all to understand, like the men of Issachar, the times in which we live and to know what we should do (1 Chronicles 12:32).

Reflection

1. Remember to look for common interests (likes, dislikes, perspectives) as you attempt to create greater openness for spiritual dialogue.

2. To find that point of intersection between your beliefs and your non-Christian friend's beliefs requires you to understand who they are and what they believe deep in their heart. This will involve a commitment on your part to take the time to really get to know them.

3. Despite your numerous disagreements with your non-Christian friends and acquaintances, always remember to work hard on bringing to the surface those things that you do agree on. Build your case for Christ one step at a time over a period of time.

4. In an age of pluralism, it's so important to communicate to our friends how much Jesus stands apart from everyone else. Help them to see by the things you say that He truly is one of a kind. Help them also to see by the way you live that same resurrection power can help those who follow Him to live different lives as well.

5. Resist the temptation to argue your point to your non-Christian friends, especially in front of other people. Don't take your eyes from the ultimate goal, which is to remove barriers so as to help others take a step closer to Christ each day. Don't win the individual battle but lose the war in your struggle for the souls of men!

6. In building your bridge with others, you may want to ask questions that help your nonbelieving friends acknowledge the truth of each plank. That way they surface the truth

for themselves rather than have you tell them what they should believe.

7. Our biggest problem in witnessing effectively today is not a problem of methodology but of maturity. If we truly care about God and want to extend His purposes in the world, we will develop a kingdom mentality that makes the most of every conversation, every day, with those who come across our path.

Application

1. Write down the apologetic outline (mentioned in this chapter) and record your understanding of each point. Ask the Lord to help you more fully grasp these basic truths as you earnestly study Scripture (2 Timothy 3:16-17) and read other apologetic resources to better equip you to answer the questions people ask.

2. Ask your spouse or a friend to listen to your logical presentation of the case for Christianity. Ask for constructive feedback on what you said and what they think you should have said.

3. Think back to the conversations you've had with those on your "top three list." Ask yourself what is the most effective way to build common ground with each one (remember this may vary from individual to individual). Once you've determined where your friends' beliefs and your beliefs intersect, record your observations under step 4 in appendix 1.

4. Determine what planks to use to construct your bridge to the Gospel with your "top three." Ask yourself what planks they will more easily accept that could lead to other planks that may help them take a step closer to Christ. Record your ideas under step 4 in appendix 1.

5. Also determine what kind of bridges (*heart* or *head*) will be most effective in witnessing to your "top three." Record your ideas under step 4 in the appropriate spaces.

6. Now that you've recorded all your observations in appendix 1, read again what you recorded as well as review the points listed in appendix 2. Now think and pray about what might be the most effective strategy for witnessing to your "top three." Don't rush this reflection. Take your time. When you think you have some good ideas, record your insights under step 4 in appendix 1.

7. Examine the depth of your relationship with Christ and seek Him fervently. Not only is this what the Christian is called to do, but your deep relationship with Christ will profoundly affect your witness to others.

8. Ask the Lord to guide you to initiate a dialogue with other nonbelievers (not necessarily your "top three"). Use the same process you used with those on your top three list. Then be willing to go wherever the Lord directs you and to say what He wants you to say!

Chapter 7

The Art of Asking Questions of People with Different Worldviews

David: So you believe that what the terrorists did in blowing up the World Trade Center and killing all those people was definitely wrong?

Student: Yes, I do, and I really believe in my heart that some day they will be held accountable for the things they've done!

David: Really? But I thought you told me you don't believe in an afterlife?

Student: Yes, that's true. Humans have come about only as a by-product of matter and energy plus time and chance.

David: But if you don't believe in an afterlife, then you can't believe in any kind of heaven or hell, right?

Student: Yes, that's correct.

David: So then please tell me, how is it possible that the terrorists are going to be held accountable for their actions, not during their lifetime but after this life is over, when you don't believe in a next life? If you don't believe in any kind of place of punishment after this life is over, where people like Hitler or the terrorists can be punished for the horrible acts they've committed, how are the terrorists going to be held accountable?

Student: I don't know…

Skills to Master in Removing Barriers to the Gospel

In our postmodern world, Christians need to master certain skills in order to remove barriers to reach others with the Gospel, something the Bible instructs us to do (2 Corinthians 10:5; 1 Peter 3:15; Jude 3). We need to learn how to ask the right questions to help others reconsider their beliefs and create in them a greater interest to learn more about Jesus.

Barriers to Removing Barriers

The difficulty today in removing barriers to the Gospel is amplified by several factors. First, our beliefs go against the postmodern grain. Consequently, it is important that we know not only what to say to people, but also how to say it. We must not come across as know-it-alls, but as one beggar telling another beggar where to find bread. We need to learn how to give an answer with meekness and fear (1 Peter 3:15 NKJV).

Second, our beliefs are assimilated into other religious beliefs. In the East, Jesus becomes one additional god in a pantheon of gods who can help us with our problems. In both East and West, many think there is no real difference between Christianity and other religions. In the West, Christianity is considered no better than most other religious beliefs. It may be perceived as one of the ways to God, but certainly not the only way.

Third, relativism has become increasingly more effective in hindering the proclamation of the truth. Pointing out the inconsistencies in others' beliefs has been misunderstood as arrogance and intolerance. Our confident knowledge of the truth causes nonbelievers to shun us and makes their walls harder to penetrate. We must be careful in our dialogue with others to not come across as argumentative, boastful, arrogant, condescending, or insensitive.

We must learn to ask questions in the most prudent way so that our dialogue is constructive, keeping in mind the threefold goals in using questions in the Conversational Evangelism model. We need to learn to ask questions in a way that surfaces *uncertainty* in others' perspectives, minimizes their *defensiveness,* and yet creates in them a *curiosity* to want to hear more.

Tips to Removing Barriers

The following seven tips may be helpful to consider as we attempt to more effectively reach our postmodern generation for Christ.

1. Work through issues with others on their timetable.

We need to ask questions and help our friends work through issues on their own timetable, not ours. If they perceive our dialogue with them as "selling" because we expect them to make an immediate decision, they will view this in a negative light. It may be a long, hard journey before some people ever seriously consider the person of Christ. Consequently, we need to be patient with people as we help them work through the discrepancies in their perspective. Real progress may take time.

Christian evangelist Nick Pollard reminds us why it is so important to cultivate this attitude.

> Many of the students I am seeking to help day by day are nowhere near ready to become Christians. Nor do they even want to hear about Jesus…With these people my immediate goal is not to see them become Christians…nor is it even to see them take one step closer to Jesus; often we are not quite in that ball park either. My goal is just to help them to take one step further away from their current worldview.[1]

Changing ways of thinking is just as slow as changing behavior, and we need to adjust our perspective accordingly in witnessing to postmoderns. Some things just take time.

2. Understand their worldview perspective.

One of the main difficulties in Conversational Evangelism is determining which questions will be the most effective. We must base our dialogue on the perspectives of the hearer. People have differing world-views, and those views should help us determine the questions to ask.

This is a biblical and prudent approach. For example, in Mark 2:1-12 Jesus knew the Pharisees believed that only God could heal and forgive sins. Consequently, He said to the paralytic, "Son, your sins are forgiven," and then healed him physically in order to confront these religious leaders with the truth of who He was. In Acts 28:23 Paul explained how the Old Testament Scriptures, prophecies, and the Law of Moses pointed to Christ because he knew his audience accepted these Scriptures. In Acts 17:28-29 Paul spoke to a group of Epicurean and Stoic philosophers and showed how their beliefs were inconsistent with some of their own writers and poets.

How we dialogue with others will depend on their worldview. With an atheist we may have to start from a different place than we would with someone who believes in theism. With an atheist in our postmodern world, we may first have to explain why we believe in absolutes. For example, postmoderns may accept contradictory statements about the existence of God. They may say things like, "He may exist for you, but He doesn't exist for me." If we do not establish the foundation for truth, we may find ourselves more and more having conversations that don't really get anywhere.

After establishing the existence of absolute truth, we may have to explain next why we believe that God exists before we can talk about Christ. Why argue that Jesus is the Son of God with those who believe there is no God to begin with? One student confessed to me, "Even if you could prove to me that Jesus rose from the dead, it does not prove that Jesus is God. In a naturalistic world, Jesus' resurrection would just be considered an anomaly." Logically this student had a point, even though he may have known that what he was saying was mere speculation or at worst pure fabrication.

The same is true if you are talking to a Hindu. You may not be able to talk about Jesus with him or her without first explaining what kind of God you are talking about. This is not necessary when speaking to

Muslims. A Muslim already believes in a theistic God, though he does not believe that Jesus ever claimed to be God. We probably need to start by talking about the reliability and authority of the Bible before he may consider what we say about Jesus. An Asian person influenced by Hinduism, Taoism, or animistic beliefs may blend worldviews by claiming Jesus is one of the many gods within their pantheon.

When we talk about different perspectives, we are speaking about different *worldviews*.

> A worldview is a way of viewing or interpreting all of reality. It is an interpretive framework through which or by which one makes sense out of the data of life and the world…For example, an orthodox Jew looks at the exodus of Israel from Egypt as a divine intervention. He sees it as a miracle. A naturalist, on the other hand, would view the same event (if it really happened) as an anomaly, that is, as an unusual natural event.[2]

So the questions we ask our nonbelieving friends depend on the worldviews they hold. Evangelist Nick Pollard says, "If I am to help people who are not interested in looking at Jesus because they are quite happy with what they believe, I must first set about understanding what it is that they believe. I must do everything I can to understand their worldview. Only then will I know what kinds of questions to raise with them."[3]

The worldviews others hold *color* how they see reality. I remember a number of years ago talking to a Hindu graduate student about the evidence for the resurrection of Jesus Christ. After I finished explaining some of the more important evidences, she looked me squarely in the eyes and said, "I believe we all have the power to do what Jesus did." She was reinterpreting the evidence of the resurrection through her worldview of pantheism. Her worldview colored how she saw the evidence. In the same way, our nonbelieving friends' worldviews color how they perceive reality.

Understanding what is coloring others' perspectives will help us know what kinds of questions would be most helpful in dialoguing with them.

This will also help minimize our disagreements because we will be more aware of how certain presuppositions influence their conclusions. Our questions will be directed to help them see this truth. Paul Copan says, "A Hindu or a New Ager, who approaches reality from a pantheistic point of view, may believe that human problems arise from ignorance—ignorance of one's own divinity or of the illusory nature of the physical world. A Christian, however, sees sin and its consequent separation from a holy God as the source of the human problem."[4] It is important to remember this as we seek to facilitate a more fruitful discussion.

Now in our witness, it may not always be necessary to establish the theistic worldview prior to discussing the evidence for Jesus as the promised Messiah. The Bible teaches that God has inscribed the moral law on people's hearts (Romans 2:14-15), whether they admit it or not. Furthermore, Ecclesiastes 3:11 reminds us that God has set "eternity in the hearts of men." Also Romans 1:18-20 reminds us that people do know something about God from nature, but they suppress that knowledge. They are ignorant because they do not desire to know God even though it is possible for them to know something about Him (Ephesians 4:18).

So while it may be logically necessary to first establish the theistic worldview perspective to make a strong case for Christianity, it may not always be practically necessary. Furthermore, it is often counterproductive to raise questions our nonbelieving friends are not asking. We should deal with worldview issues only if it is apparent that their worldview is so radically different from ours that it makes it difficult to find common ground. For while it is unadvisable to go into battle with a peashooter, we should also never go to target practice with a bazooka! We should determine what kind of apologetic ammunition is appropriate to the situation. By observing this approach to the use of apologetics, we may find that it increases the effectiveness of our witness to others.

Mix and Matching Worldviews. Remember, it is difficult for others to change their perspective. People often choose beliefs based on how they want to look at the world. They believe what they want to believe so they can do what they want to do! This is especially true of college students.

Furthermore, the more they behave a certain way, the more their view of the world is reinforced. Nick Pollard says,

> As individuals develop, they do seem to adopt certain answers to the fundamental questions of life. These answers are put together into a comprehensive system—a view of the world. At the same time, however, this view of the world becomes the way they view the world. It becomes the spectacles through which they look, the grid upon which they organize reality. This view affects the way they answer the fundamental questions of life, and so on. If we understand worldviews this way, we can see why they are so hard to change. They tend to become firmly entrenched because they constantly reinforce themselves through the self-sustaining feedback loop.[5]

Many people mix and match their worldviews according to how they want to believe (note the conversation at the beginning of this chapter). Postmodern people mix worldviews in two ways. Pollard calls these the "Bottom-up" and "Top-down" models. A "bottom-up" model describes "the conclusions that a person comes to after looking at the world and asking the most fundamental questions about it: 'Who am I?' 'Where am I?' 'What's wrong with the world?' and 'What's the remedy?'" A top-down model, on the other hand, is "the point from which they start. It is the way people view the world, the spectacles through which they look, the grid upon which they organize reality."[6]

Most postmodern people choose a top-down approach to worldviews. They are drawn to believe something because it allows them to justify their questionable behavior, not because they believe it is true. When they encounter ideas that contradict their view, how do they respond? Pollard offers this insightful answer: "Given that our young person already holds a set of contradictory beliefs, it is not a problem for her to adopt one more, even if it makes absolute claims or demands, provided she is not alerted to this. She is already managing to ignore one set of contradictions, so one more is not going to make much difference."[7]

This worldview confusion then leads to a buffet approach to beliefs. People pick those beliefs that are compatible with how they want to live.

This worldview mixing makes it difficult to determine what their perspective is and what kinds of questions to ask. How can we determine a person's particular viewpoint? Pollard says, "Essentially this is a 'pattern-matching process.' I have in my mind a large number of contemporary worldviews and know the kinds of beliefs and values to which they lead. Then I consider the beliefs and values being expressed by a person, and I look for the best match (or selection of matches) to identify the underlying worldview or worldviews."[8]

To determine others' perspectives in the West, we need to know the basic characteristics of naturalism, nihilism, existentialism, deism, theism, pantheism, and postmodernism. In Eastern cultures it is also helpful to understand animism, Buddhism, and Taoism. Most people embrace one of three major worldviews: theism, pantheism, and atheism. Theists (includes adherents of Judaism, Christianity, and Islam) believe that God made all. Pantheists (includes adherents of some forms of Buddhism, Hinduism, and the New Age movement) believe that God is all. Atheists do not believe in God at all.

Even without much knowledge of these varying worldviews, you can uncover much about your friends' perspectives by continuing to ask probing questions to clarify their beliefs. This will provide you with the data that will help you discern the questions to ask to surface the discrepancies in their perspective. This will build a bridge for further dialogue.

3. Encourage them to question whether their foundation is adequate.

People are seldom motivated to change their beliefs. Consequently, we need to help our friends question whether their worldview foundation is adequate. We do this by asking probing questions rather than telling them what to believe. Pollard concurs with this approach:

> I have some information which I want to communicate to them. I want to do it in such a way that I encourage them to think, question and come to their own conclusion. This usually means giving them information in the form of a question rather than a statement. There is no set, pat approach, but I often use phrases such as, "I can see a lot of truth in that, but have you thought about…?"[9]

At least two practical measuring sticks will help others evaluate whether their beliefs are adequate. First, ask them to determine if their beliefs are consistently *affirmable*. If a belief is not affirmable, it cannot be true! Webster says to *affirm* something is "to say something and be willing to stand by its truth." Something may be "sayable" but not necessarily affirmable. I can *say* that I cannot speak a word of English, but I cannot meaningfully *affirm* this truth. I cannot meaningfully affirm something to be true while denying it in the very process of making the statement. "No statement is true if, in order to make it, the opposite would have to be true."[10] For example, the statement that we cannot know anything about ultimate reality is unaffirmable because in making the statement we are claiming to know something about ultimate reality. That is why beliefs like nihilism are unaffirmable. For someone to claim that no meaning or value exists, they must at least value the right to express their belief.

Pantheism is also unaffirmable as a worldview because it says that God exists but we as individual people do not. Yet a person must exist in order to make the statement that God exists and he does not. Atheism is also unaffirmable. "One cannot meaningfully affirm that reality has no ultimate meaning (as in God) without thereby making the claim that his statement is ultimately meaningful about reality."[11]

Every other worldview apart from theism is unaffirmable.[12] Theism is affirmable and therefore true because it not only does not contradict itself, but also because it corresponds to reality and is therefore *undeniable*.[13] So if a worldview cannot be meaningfully affirmed, then it cannot be true. This is the first measuring stick we can use to help others evaluate the strength of their beliefs.

The second measuring stick is the principle of *livability*.[14] If our view of reality corresponds to the truth, it should also be livable. If something is true, it must be livable. Yet the reverse is not necessarily true since something that seems livable may not necessarily be true. One may claim that some Buddhist beliefs are livable in some way, but those beliefs are not true. Yet a pantheistic view that ultimate reality is beyond good and evil is certainly unlivable.

One of the questions I ask college students who claim to hold to a pantheistic framework is, "Why do you believe one way and yet live another?" Most ask me to clarify what I mean. I tell them that if ultimate reality is one, then it must be beyond good and evil because otherwise there would be at least two realities. Yet most pantheists live their lives with the internal belief that certain things are right or wrong. So while pantheism makes no distinction between love and cruelty, a person may find it difficult to live this way.[15] Furthermore, if reality is ultimately one, then the plurality we observe in life is an illusion. Yet the pantheist does not live his life as though there is one reality. He makes a distinction between right and wrong and lives his life in a way that assumes there is plurality. So what a pantheist says he believes does not match up with how he lives.

We can use these two measuring sticks—"Is your belief system consistently affirmable?" and "Is your belief system in fact livable?"—to help others consider the adequacy of their beliefs.

4. Focus your questions on those things that stand out the most.

Unfortunately, some make the mistake of using apologetics like a hammer and wonder why it is ineffective. It is not effective to try to change a person's behavior by pointing out all the ways he has not measured up. As we mentioned before, we should not point out all the inconsistencies in our spouses' viewpoint during a disagreement. That will just make them more defensive and cause them to pull back emotionally from us. Instead, we should gently express our *major* concerns and highlight a few of the discrepancies in their statements that seem obvious to us, hoping that they see the discrepancies as well.

In the same way, when witnessing to nonbelievers, wisdom teaches us to point out just a few key things we would like them to think about. We should not dump our truckload all at once. The flesh may lead us to pounce on people and show them why they are wrong and we are right. But we need the Holy Spirit to lead us to discern when, where, and how to use apologetic tools.

We need to be strategic in what questions we ask and how we ask them. This is especially true in an age that sees reasoning as overly argumentative. Those we speak to can become easily defensive and cut off any further dialogue with us. It is important then that others see us as an ally who is trying to help them work through their struggles rather than as an enemy they feel obligated to attack, even if they agree with some of what we say.

5. *Understand some of the basic evidence for the Christian faith.*

Memorize the 12 steps in the Apologetic Outline discussed in chapter 6. Learning how to use these 12 steps to establish the case for Christianity can play an important role in pinpointing the most pressing objection a person may have about the Christian faith. It helps us to know where that person is in the overall argument for Christianity, and we can see if we need to go back to a previous point to establish it more firmly. Otherwise, we may not be able to move that person along to the conclusion of the argument.

For example, if a person is not buying the argument for the historicity of the New Testament (point 6), it may be that he does not really believe miracles are possible (point 4). And if he is having problems with accepting miracles, it is probably because he is not firmly convinced that a theistic God exists (point 3), and so on. So knowing the overall argument will help us pinpoint the problem and return to the premise needed to get that person over the hump.

6. *Identify some key questions to ask.*

It is also helpful to memorize some key questions to ask when speaking to people with different viewpoints. In appendix 5, we've listed a number of questions that you should consider using in your witness to an atheist, agnostic, Muslim, Hindu, Buddhist, or Taoist.

7. *Ask God for wisdom.*

"If any of you lacks wisdom, he should ask God, who gives generously to all without finding fault, and it will be given to him" (James 1:5). Because we do not always understand the underlying issues people are struggling with, it is especially important to ask the Holy Spirit for wisdom to help us discern what questions to ask and when. Remember that God is the great physician. If we can discern His diagnosis, we can give the person the proper medication.

Conclusion

These seven tips—work through issues with others on their timetable, understand their perspective, encourage them to question whether their foundation is adequate, focus our questions on those things that stand out the most, understand some of the basic evidence for the Christian faith, identify some key questions to ask, and ask the Holy Spirit for wisdom—are helpful in more effectively using the Conversational Evangelism model to reach those in the new millennium. Engaging others with sensitivity to these issues could play an important part in helping them reevaluate their beliefs and may provide the motivation they need to take another look at Jesus.

Reflection

1. Witnessing is more difficult today partly because our Christian beliefs go radically against the grain of our culture. We not only need to know what to say to people, but also how to communicate it so that we receive the greatest possibility of our message being heard and accepted.

2. We must especially be careful not to come across as argumentative, boastful, arrogant, condescending, or insensitive. We must also learn to ask questions in the most prudent way so that our dialogue is constructive.

3. The best way to determine which questions will be the most effective in witnessing to our nonbelieving friends is to understand their worldview perspective.

4. Different underlying worldview assumptions can account for differences in perspectives and can lead to strong disagreements. So your friend may look at the evidence you present to him and come to radically different conclusions. Keep this in mind if you reach an impasse in your discussion with someone.

5. Finding the right question to ask to surface the discrepancies in people's religious beliefs is not always easy when

they mix worldviews together and don't hold their religious views consistently.

6. Though some people might dispute the existence of definite or absolute right and wrong (as opposed to relative right and wrong), remember that their lives are full of decisions based on right vs. wrong, correct vs. incorrect, moral vs. immoral.

7. Remember that in an age of relativism, the two measuring sticks that can still be used to distinguish truth from error are whether something is consistently *affirmable* and whether it is *livable*.

8. While not required, it is helpful to understand non-Christian beliefs prior to witnessing to those of other faiths. Not only will your confidence increase, you will better know how to ask probing questions that more effectively surface their discrepancies. Start by acquiring and carefully reading one of the recommended resources listed at the back of this book.

9. Given the rapid spread of Islam, take the time to correctly understand the most important beliefs of this religion, whether in reading about it or, better yet, talking to a Muslim. In the same way, seek to accurately understand other non-Christian faiths.

Application

1. How we dialogue with others will depend on their worldview. Therefore, make a mental list of the worldview perspectives you hear in your conversations with your non-Christian friends. Considering that they may not always be consistent, which worldview category do most of their beliefs fall into?

2. The next time you run into a snag in your witness to someone who holds to a radically different religious perspective, consider building your case for Christ a few steps further back in the 12-step approach you learned for establishing the case for Christianity.

3. Reflect on what basis you make the various decisions in your life. Then explore the consequences of deliberately making decisions as though it really makes no difference which way you decided. For example, consider whether there would be any consequences for thinking that there is no absolute right or wrong in making the decision to download copyrighted music or videos. To make you more effective in your witness to postmoderns, integrate the insights you gain in trying to apply relativistic thinking to help you better understand how a relativist thinks.

4. Begin to memorize some of the key questions from appendix 5. Next time you have an opportunity, ask one of those questions of your friend who holds to one of those beliefs (atheism, agnosticism, Buddhism, Hinduism, Islam). Remember to reword the question in language you are comfortable with.

5. Begin to memorize the key points of the Apologetic Outline (see chapter 6). In your discussions with others, try to ask questions in a way that will allow your friends to surface the truth for themselves, yet come to the same conclusions that you hold. Learn to string question after question in such a way that you build common beliefs with each question asked and answered. Memorizing the key points will help you to not skip those that may help others discover that Christianity truly is a reasonable faith and that knowing God can be a great spiritual adventure.

Chapter 8

The Art of Answering Objections
While Moving Forward

Student: You know, I've got to be honest with you. I know that everything you're telling me about Jesus is true. But I've just got some things in my life I don't want to give up!

David: I really appreciate your honesty. I find a lot of times I have conversations with college students who aren't really honest with me about what's standing in the way of them accepting Christ. Your honesty is so refreshing to hear.

Student: Well, I know how annoyed I get when people try to pull one over on me.

David: Let me offer you one perspective about how to think about your situation. You see, God doesn't expect us to get our lives cleaned up before we make the decision to follow Christ. We must first decide that we're going in the wrong direction and then ask God for the desire to want to turn around and move in the opposite direction. Then we must also ask Him for the ability to do what we know we would never be able to do in our own strength.

All the things that you and I may think are so important

to hold onto in this life, someday we'll realize how insignificant they are compared to what's going to happen in the next life. Jim Elliot, who was a martyred missionary, probably said it best. "He is no fool to give up what he cannot keep to gain what he cannot lose."

The Problem in Just Answering Nonbelievers' Stated Questions

We need to learn how to provide solid answers to nonbelievers' frequently asked questions, but we need to do so in a way that encourages them to overcome their obstacles and take one step closer to Christ. But we are not really helping them to go further in their spiritual journey unless we can answer not only their questions but also answer questions *behind* the questions they ask us. This is not an easy art to master.

Understanding the Nature of Their Barrier

One way to ensure that our approach will yield the greatest amount of fruit is to determine the nature of their barrier to Christ and then develop a remedy to clear up their confusion. There are at least *two kinds* of general barriers that people have to the Gospel—barriers to their *understanding* of Christianity and barriers to their *embracing* of Christianity. Although people may have a mixture of the two, usually one will be more prominent than the other.

For example, we have met people who say, "I know what you're telling me about Christ is true, but I want to live life my way." These people aren't confused about what is involved in being a Christian—they don't have many obstacles in their understanding of Christianity (though most likely they have some). Their real problem is that they have obstacles in wanting to embrace Christianity. Some obstacles to embracing Christianity might be:

- Their sinful and selfish nature (Jeremiah 17:9)
- Their indifference toward religious perspectives
- Their focus on materialism

- Their negative attitude toward Christianity's claim to be the only way to God
- Their pluralistic mind-set that encourages them to keep their options open
- Hypocrisy among Christians

Then there are those who by their words show they don't have a clear understanding of Christianity. To them, it's just a religion of dos and don'ts. Because they don't have a clear understanding of what Christianity is all about, they don't have any desire to embrace it. Examples of obstacles in their understanding of Christianity are:

- Thinking there is no difference between religious beliefs
- Not understanding the nature of sin and its consequences
- Not understanding the meaning of salvation by grace (believing rather in salvation by works)
- Not being able to reconcile the problem of evil with the existence of a loving God

Asking the Four Questions Behind Each Question

The more effective we are in identifying common barriers and removing false understandings, the more we will be able to help others take one step closer to Jesus Christ. To clarify misunderstandings and build bridges to the Gospel, we need to ask and answer at least *four fundamental questions* for each major question our nonbelieving friends may ask us:

1. What are the possible questions (or issues) behind each question (or issue) that needs to be addressed?
2. What terms that they use need to be clarified?
3. What truth do we want them to grasp about the question or issue raised?
4. What questions and illustrations can we use to help them grasp this truth?

It is especially important to use illustrations and stories if we are going to increase our chances of being heard in today's postmodern culture. Evangelist Nick Pollard reminds us of two major characteristics of postmodernism that are important to keep in mind: the emphasis on questioning and the displacement of propositional truth in favor of stories.[1] Consequently, we should use questions, stories, and illustrations in our dialogue with our nonbelieving friends.

A college student with a Hindu background asked me, "Why aren't my good works good enough to get me into heaven?" and "Why can't God just let me into heaven?" Now the real question behind those questions was, "Is God really just and fair in His dealings with mankind?" The theological truth I wanted him to grasp is this: As human beings we tend to overestimate our own righteousness and underestimate God's holiness. But to effectively communicate this, I needed to allow him to surface this truth for himself by asking him questions and using stories to illustrate my point.

I noticed he was drinking a cup of water so I asked him, "Would it be acceptable to put a little sewage in your water?"

Of course he said no.

"So you see how something can seem so small yet in reality can still have a huge impact? In a similar way we look at our sins and see them as no big deal, and yet from God's point of view they have a big impact on our relationship with Him. So do you see how it's possible that our sins could cause a bigger barrier between us and God than we think?"

Here's another illustration you could use to make the same point. "Picture a young woman getting out of a car in her beautiful white wedding dress.[2] Then imagine another car pulling up right next to her and a man with grease all over him gets out. As he passes by her, he smears grease all over her beautiful white wedding dress. Now, do you think that wedding dress is going to be acceptable to her? Obviously not, because any woman can tell you that a white wedding dress has to be spotless! If you and I have a standard of what is right and wrong, and we do not live up to it, can you imagine that God's standard might be a little higher than our own?"

Notice that we do not declare what God's standard is (Matthew 5:48;

James 2:10); we merely try to get them to realize the possibility of God's standards, thus building common ground with them.

Doing More than Providing an Answer

We also need to do more than answer nonbelievers' real questions if we're going to have a greater impact on our friends. We need to provide solid answers to their questions, yet do it in a way that will help build bridges to the cross. One day, I had an opportunity to talk to an elderly lady who asked, "Is it true that we're all going to be judged after this life is over?" Now in asking this question she might have really been wondering, "Is God really fair for sending people to hell?" or "Should God be punishing me even when I do my very best?"

Now remember, in answering their questions and the possible questions behind their questions, we also want to provide an answer in a way that will help them take steps toward Christ. So one possible way to answer her would be to say, "Yes, it's true that none of us measure up to either God's standard or even our own standard of right and wrong. So God is just in His dealings with us." But then to build a bridge with this person we should also say, "But the good news is that God has provided an answer to our dilemma by sending Jesus..."

We should always try to find a way to help others take a step closer with each conversation or question they ask us. In doing this, we are remembering our goal to remove obstacles to the cross (2 Corinthians 10:5). Now with the four questions and goal in mind, let's look at some frequent questions we are asked and give some suggestions for answering them.

Key Questions to Answer Using the Conversational Evangelism Approach

Certain key questions or objections emerge from nonbelievers in our generation. Whether real or imaginary, they are barriers to reaching people for Christ. We need ready answers to tear down these obstacles to the Gospel in a way that doesn't make nonbelievers feel torn down as well. The following are some of the more common questions/objections that emerge.

1. It doesn't matter what you believe as long as you are sincere and you don't hurt anyone else. There is ample experience to verify that people can be sincerely wrong. We do it all the time when we make a wrong turn in traffic. The same is true in other areas of life. Further, being sincerely wrong may be fatal. If we skate on what we think is thick ice and fall through, it can be disastrous. Sincerely believing a blinking light at a railroad crossing is just stuck can be fatal if we cross and a train is coming.

The questions behind this statement about sincerity need to be addressed. Sincerely believing without evidence or against the evidence is not a wise course of action in any area of life, let alone one with eternal consequences. Also, we need to determine what terms we might want to clarify with them. For example, we may want to ask,

- "What do you mean by being *sincere*? Does sincerity guarantee you a good outcome?"
- "How would you define what it means to *not hurt* someone?"
- "How do you know that your beliefs will not harm someone in some way?"

We ask these questions because we want them to grasp an important truth: It is not our sincerity but the object of our belief that is important.

Finally, we need to emphasize that sincerity is no safeguard to the truth, and use something like the following to illustrate our point: "I'm sure the terrorists of 9/11 were sincere in what they believed, but they were sincerely wrong." Then to build a bridge, we can ask: "If it does really matter what we believe (because not all views are equally valid), how do you personally determine who is right and who is wrong?" Asking this question in this way could lead to greater spiritual openness to hear about our Jesus.

2. What's so special about Christianity? I thought that all religions basically teach the same thing.

The truth we want nonbelievers to grasp is that not all religious leaders make the same claims and have the same weight of evidence to verify those claims. What then are some questions or illustrations we can use to help them grasp this truth?

We could ask them, "Are you aware that all religions do not teach the same thing? Christians believe that salvation is accomplished by faith alone in Christ alone. Muslims believe that salvation is accomplished by belief in Allah, his prophet Muhammad, and good works—that their good works have to outweigh their bad works. Most Hindus believe that salvation is accomplished by overcoming karma and incarnations with good works. Buddhists believe that salvation comes by cessation of desire through an eight-fold path."

To help them see that all religions do not teach the same things, ask, "Would you agree that Jesus either is the promised Messiah or He is not? If He is the promised Messiah, then those who strictly follow Judaism are wrong. If He is not the promised Messiah, then Christians are wrong."

The bottom line is that not all beliefs can be right because they mutually exclude each other.

Another question to help nonbelievers see the truth is: "Are you aware that comparing Christianity to the world's religions is not like comparing apples with apples? Christ's claims and proof of those claims are unique compared to any other major religious leader. Buddha claimed to point to the way, Muhammad claimed to be a prophet of God, but Jesus Christ is the only major religious leader who ever claimed to be God, fulfilled prophecy, lived a sinless life, and then died on the cross and rose from the dead."

One day I had a conversation with a Chinese lady and found out that her mother was a Buddhist and her sister was a Christian. She was trying to figure out which one to believe. So I asked her, "If you were coming to the end of your life, and you met Jesus and other great religious leaders and each suggested a different path, whose advice should you take? Wouldn't you take the advice of someone who's been to the other side and came back to tell us about it?" In asking her those questions, I was able to remove an obstacle in her mind that Christianity was just as good but no better than any other religious belief.

A few weeks later I asked her, "If you were not sure if you should follow Jesus or other great religious leaders, consider this perspective. If you follow Jesus and you are wrong, you may have many other lifetimes to get it right. But if you follow other paths and you are wrong, you don't have any more chances to get it right. Wouldn't it be wise then to choose Christ first?"

In asking the question in this way, I was helping to build a bridge to the Gospel.

3. How can you claim there is only one way to God? Are you not being arrogant and exclusive?

First, we need to ask *what might be the issue* (belief) behind this question. Nonbelievers may believe that Christians think they alone have the truth and are therefore better than others. Furthermore, they may believe that Christians are not very open to other faiths. Recognizing these beliefs, we can attempt to build a bridge by saying, "I agree with you that we should not be arrogant about our beliefs or think that we are somehow better than others who hold different beliefs. I look at Christianity as one beggar telling another beggar where to find bread."

Next, we want to *clarify the terms* they use. We could ask, for example, "What do you mean by *exclusive*?" Ravi Zacharias says, "What does the person mean by 'You must be open to everything'? What it almost always means is, 'You must be open to everything that I am open to and disagree with anything I disagree with.'"[3]

Next, we want to *address the truth we want them to grasp* (and in this case, there are several). First, for some things there may be only one way, and second, exclusiveness is not necessarily a bad thing. The question also seems to demonstrate a lack of understanding that our lives really do need serious mending. So to help them to uncover this fact, it could be helpful to ask, "Do you think we live up to our own standards of right and wrong?" If someone is honest with himself, he must admit that he does not live up to his own standards. Then ask, "Can you see how that might cause a problem?"

Then we can use an illustration to show that for some things there may be only one way. Ask, "How many ways does it take to restore a broken relationship with a spouse or significant other for something we said or did?[4] Do we not have to say in some way that we are sorry for the things we said or did that hurt the other person? Now, if that is the way it is in our relationship with other people, why would it be any different in our relationship with God?"

Then to help them understand that exclusiveness is not necessarily a bad thing, we can ask, "When we get married, is it not true that we exclude every other person of the opposite sex to have an intimate relationship with? Do you agree that this is a good thing for us to do in our marriage?" So exclusiveness can be a very good thing depending on what we are including in our life and why, and what we are excluding and why.

But not only are Christians called arrogant and exclusive but also intolerant. To dismantle this false belief, we could ask the following:

- "Is it not possible for a Christian to believe something very different and still be tolerant of other people's beliefs?"
- "Would you agree that you are not intolerant of me when you reject my viewpoint?"
- "Is there not a difference between *discrimination* and *disagreement*?"
- "Is it judgmental to think someone is wrong?" (It is especially important that we clarify this point since tolerance is highly valued in our postmodern culture.)

4. What about those who have never heard the Gospel?

This question is not usually an attempt to wrestle with deep theological issues but rather is a smoke screen to avoid the truth of the Gospel. Once we provide an adequate answer (see below for some possible ways to address this), it is also helpful to turn the question around (using the boomerang principle) so they feel a responsibility to do something with our answer. To do this we can ask, "Now that you know, what are you going to do about this problem?" In this way we are encouraging them to take a step closer to Christ.

In answering the question it is helpful to determine whether there might be an issue or question behind the question, such as, "How is it fair for God to condemn someone for not having enough knowledge to save him, but just enough knowledge to condemn him?"⁵

To answer this, we must remember that God is not responsible to give us greater light of who He is when we have not responded to the light we already have. Matthew 13:12 says, "Whoever has will be given more." Other examples of this in Scripture are the Ethiopian in Acts 8, Cornelius in Acts 10, and God-fearing Greeks in Acts 17. Romans 1 teaches us that all people have some knowledge about God, even if it is not saving knowledge.

Consider this illustration that demonstrates how God is still just even if men never come to know anything about Jesus Christ. Suppose you are lost in a desert and it is getting dark. You are hungry, thirsty, and know that if you do not find food and shelter soon, you are probably going to die. Then you see a speck of light on the horizon indicating that there is human life out there. If you move away from the light instead of toward it, whose fault is it if you die? It would be your fault, right? Had you chosen to move toward the light, would not the light have grown brighter, revealing who was there? In a similar way, God is not responsible to give us greater light if we have not responded to the light He has already provided through general revelation.

Furthermore, the Bible shows us God's universal concern for mankind when it tells us that there will be people "from every nation, tribe, people and language" in heaven (Revelation 7:9), which proves that God is not discriminatory in His love and desires for all to come to know Him (2 Peter 3:9).

Finally, it is helpful to ask, "If God really loved us and demonstrated it by paying the ultimate price in sending Jesus to die in our place, is it not possible He would be willing to do whatever it took to save us?" After this question, we can again ask them the key question: "What are you going to do with this information since you know about Christ?"

5. *It's okay to believe what you want as long as you don't try to convert others to your beliefs.*

First, we need to determine the belief behind the question. Nonbelievers may think trying to change someone's beliefs demonstrates arrogance and narrow-mindedness. You should ask for clarification about what they mean by *convert*. Some additional questions to ask are:

- "Do you believe that persuading someone to change their mind is always wrong? Persuasion can be a good thing in certain circumstances, right?"
- "How do you determine whether persuading someone to believe something is right or wrong?"
- "Would you want to convert me to your viewpoint if you think I am wrong?"

Converting someone to another viewpoint is not always a bad thing. It might even be a loving thing to do, especially if we're talking about things that are harmful (such as drugs or smoking).

A bridge to the Gospel can be built from this point by telling a story that teaches that what matters most is that we believe the right thing, especially as it relates to our eternal destiny.

For example, several years ago I participated in a panel representing the Christian view along with panel members from other religious perspectives. Each panel member explained something about his beliefs, and each one added at the end, "But I don't think I should try to proselytize or convert others to my beliefs." I was the last to speak, and there was tremendous pressure to say something similar. So to make the point about the urgency of telling others about Christ, I asked this hypothetical question: "What if your best friend was trapped in a burning building, and you knew if you didn't try to rescue him (and you could) he was going to die. What kind of friend would you be if you just let him burn? Not a very good friend, right? I just want to warn people about the dangers of rejecting Jesus Christ." After I said this, there was such a hush you could hear a pin drop. Obviously, they had gotten the point, and the Holy Spirit was using it to penetrate their hearts.

The most loving thing you and I can ever do is to tell others the Good News that has the power to transform lives today and guarantee them a future and a hope tomorrow!

6. *Can you prove to me that God exists?*

Again, we first need to determine the belief behind the question.

They may believe that reason and logic cannot properly be applied to questions about religion and God. To surface this belief we can ask, "What do you mean by *prove?*" In an age where some question whether any reality exists, it may be difficult to give satisfactory proof that any-thing exists, including one's own existence. Yet we can ask, "Are you asking me if I can demonstrate that there are good reasons to believe that God exists?"

Once you clarify the question, you can use the boomerang principle and say, "I believe I can offer you some good reasons to believe that God does exist. But first let me ask you, if you could know that God does in fact exist, would you want to know that? If not, why not?" If they say they do not believe there is any reason to believe that God exists, you can question their skepticism with some of the following questions:

- "Is there any particular reason why you don't believe God exists?"

- "Are you telling me that you are absolutely sure there is no God? If not, then is it not possible that there is a God? If so, then are you not really an agnostic (who says, 'I don't know if there is a God') but not really an atheist (who says, 'I know that there is no God')?"

- "Can you prove for sure that there is no God? If not, then is it not possible there is a God? And if there might be a God, would it not be wise to consider what this would mean for your life and afterlife?"

- "Would you agree with me that it's difficult to explain *love, meaning, values,* and *beauty* if we are just effects from material causes?"

This latter question is helpful because even in a postmodern world people want to believe there is something meaningful in their lives beyond this material universe. This may even explain the fascination among young people for "reality TV"; they are looking for something real even though it goes against the grain of their postmodern beliefs. For many postmoderns, the closest thing they can find that is real is another human being they can "connect with" who has real hurts, real sorrows, and yet experiences real joys.

In answering their question about the evidence for God, it can also be helpful to combine the content of apologetics with a questioning approach. First, point out that the existence of God answers the most fundamental question anyone can ask, which is, "Why is there something rather than nothing?" Then ask,

- "Would you agree that something presently exists?" (mainly your existence)
- "Would you also agree that something cannot come from nothing?"[6]
- "Would you also agree that we *must* conclude, therefore, that something must have always existed because if there ever was a time when there was nothing, there would still be nothing?"[7]

Once you establish the plank of God's existence, you can lay down other planks, such as the possibility for miracles and of Jesus being who He claimed to be. These may be important steps to help some people in their journey toward Christ.

7. If God is loving, how can there be a hell?

The main truth you want nonbelievers to grasp here is that hell exists *because* God is loving. To help them understand this truth, ask these questions:

- "If heaven is a place where people worship God, and you do not enjoy doing that now, what kind of God would force you to do that for all eternity? Not a very loving God, right?"
- "Would it not be hell for God to force someone to love and worship Him?"
- "I'm sure you would agree that it would not be very loving for God to make everyone believe in Christ whether they wanted to or not."

Then you can use a marriage analogy to show that one cannot force another person to marry him or her, if the other person does not desire to make that commitment. In the same way, God's love precludes Him from forcing us to act against our will. There are no shotgun weddings in heaven.

To clarify this further, point out that there are some good reasons for the existence of hell. For example, ask:

- "How can you believe in the concept of justice if there were no punishment for wrongdoing?"

- "Do you believe Hitler received in this life all the punishment for his crimes? If not, how will Hitler and people like him be punished for all the evil they have done if there is no hell in the next life?"

If you believe you are making some progress with your friend, you can transition to a presentation of the Gospel. You can say that while the bad news is that because of our rebellion against God there is a separation between us and Him, there is good news for us because the story does not end there. Then wait for your friend to ask for further clarification about this Good News. If you sense he is ready for more, ask, "Would you like to hear more about this Good News that the Bible talks about?"

8. Why is there not more than one God?

If someone asks this question, we can use the boomerang principle and ask, "In what way do you think an all-powerful God can have limitations?" and "What can limit an all-powerful God?" The answer, of course, to both questions is…absolutely nothing! The Bible teaches that God has the power to hold all things together (Colossians 1:17). The Bible clearly teaches that there is only one God.

> "You are my witnesses. Is there any God besides me?
> No, there is no other Rock; I know not one."
> (Isaiah 44:8b)

Now to demonstrate this point rationally and not just affirm that this is a biblical teaching, we can say the following: "If there were more than one eternal unlimited being, would they not have to differ in some way? To differ by nothing (as opposed to something) is the same as saying they do not differ at all. To differ by something, one would have to have a quality that the other would not possess. Then one would be God and the other would not.[8] Therefore, there can be only one unlimited, unchanging, eternal God, not two or more."

9. How can there be a loving God when there is so much evil and suffering in the world?

First, we need to identify the key question or issue behind this question and also address why this question causes us so much difficulty. The implication of the question is that if God exists, He would not allow so much pain and suffering in the world. Yet if He does exist with this much evil, He is not truly good.

Second, we need to help our nonbelieving friends see that only the theist can provide an adequate answer to the question about evil and suffering. The agnostic does not have an answer because there is no one to direct the question to. The pantheist also cannot give an adequate answer because for him, evil is not real. But if theism is true, then the question is valid, and the theist can offer some valid answers.

Next, we want to define *evil* and *suffering* by asking them, "What do you mean by *evil*? Is it possible to know what is evil without some standard of good?"

C.S. Lewis, in his book *Mere Christianity*, pointed out the fallacy of accepting the concept of evil without also accepting the concept of good. He said, "[As an atheist] my argument against God was that the universe seemed so cruel and unjust. But how had I got this idea of just and unjust? A man does not call a line crooked unless he has some idea of a straight line. What was I comparing this universe with when I called it unjust?"[9]

So ask them,

- "Do we not measure what is evil by the standard of good rather than measure good by a standard of evil?"

- "If we say something is good or right, does that not imply a moral law? And if there is a moral law, does that not imply there is a moral lawgiver?"

The next term to clarify is *cause.* "Would a good God *cause* bad things to happen to good people or would a good God *allow* bad things to happen to good people?" This is important to clarify because the Bible teaches that "God cannot be tempted by evil, nor does he tempt anyone" (James 1:13). This then may lead to a further question: "Who then is the author of evil?"

A skeptic may argue that if God is the author of everything, and evil is something real, therefore God must be the cause of evil. The pantheist escapes this dilemma by insisting that somehow evil is not real, but this will not work for one who believes in theism and in the reality of evil.

The way to resolve this dilemma is to point out that evil is not a thing but a *lack or privation* of something. It is a privation in things.[10] Augustine said it was a "corruption."[11] Evil is a corruption of the good things that God made. Evil then is an ontological parasite. It can exist only in relationship to good. This means there is no such thing as pure evil, just as we know that there is no such thing as a totally moth-eaten garment. It does not exist. The same is true for rust on your car. Your car cannot be totally rust-eaten, otherwise it would not exist. Likewise, evil cannot exist without reference to good. To put it in theological terms, evil is like sin, which means to miss the mark, to fall short of the standard, to not measure up, or to be less than what we should be (Romans 3:23). Since evil can be defined as a privation or lack of something, it therefore does not follow that God causes evil (James 1:13-17).

In explaining that God is the cause of all creation and yet not the cause of evil, it is helpful to explain that when God created everything, He made everything perfect. One of the perfect things that God made was free creatures. Therefore, free will is the cause of evil (Genesis 3:6). Consequently, imperfection (evil) can arise from the perfect indirectly, through freedom.[12]

The question then is not, "Why would God cause bad things to happen to good people?" The question is, "Why would He *allow* them?" To answer this question, ask "Where do you want God to draw the line? For if God were to wipe out all evil from this day forward, what would be the result? Who among us would be left?"

Next, we need to uncover some possible assumptions behind this question. Some may assume that our goal in this life is to be happy rather than to know God, which will lead to happiness in the next life. In this life, many evils occur that do not produce happiness but do produce a greater knowledge of God.[13] Clarifying this issue may help resolve this tension in some people's minds.

It could also be helpful to remind them that even if we do not know God's purpose, He may still have a good purpose for evil. We know God uses evil for good purposes (Romans 8:28), and we can identify at least five purposes for Him to allow evil and suffering.

- It is necessary for character development.
- It teaches us moral consequences.
- It warns us of impending danger.
- It brings about the greater good.
- It brings about the final separation of good and evil.[14]

But this may lead to an additional question, "Why can God not get rid of evil?" It is helpful then to explain that God cannot destroy all evil without destroying the good of free choice. Nevertheless, He can and will defeat all evil without destroying free choice. The argument can be summarized in the following way:

- God is all-good and desires to defeat evil.
- God is all-powerful and is able to defeat evil.
- Evil is not yet defeated.
- Therefore, it will *one day* be defeated.

This may lead someone to ask, "Why would God create a world if He knew it was not the best possible world He could have created?" The answer is, "This fallen world is not the best possible world, but it is the best possible way to get to the best possible world."[15] The best possible world is one in which free creatures are allowed to maximize the potential for good. Yet to do so one must allow for the possibility of evil. In the parable about the wheat and the tares (Matthew 13:24-30), the master's servants are instructed to allow both to reach their maximum potential and then separate them in the end (v. 30). In this way the good can be maximized, while at the same time allowing evil to coexist until one day it will be quarantined forever (Revelation 20:10).

10. How can I choose Christ when my dead ancestors are separated from Him and could be separated from me?

This question reflects one of the most difficult barriers to Christ in cultures that practice ancestral worship. Consequently, it is highly critical that we give a well thought-out answer to this. Here are some suggestions.

First, we can ask, "Are you absolutely sure your ancestors are separated from Christ?" We may think we know someone's spiritual condition, but we see only the exterior, whereas God sees the heart (1 Samuel 16:7).

It is also important to realize what we should not say. We should not ask questions like, "Why would you allow someone else's decision to affect your eternal happiness?" In cultures where ancestral worship is prominent, this question would not be helpful because decisions usually are not based on what is best for the individual but on how it affects the rest of the family. Decisions that are based on individual wants and desires are perceived as very selfish in the East. Consequently, a couple of helpful questions that take family sensitivities into account are,

- "If your dead ancestors know what you know about who Jesus is, what would they advise you to do?"

- "Did you know that Scripture actually speaks to this issue? In Luke 16 Jesus tells the parable of a rich man who pleads with a beggar named Lazarus, who had died, to warn his brothers about hell."

This may then surface the question, "How can we be happy in heaven when we have a loved one in hell?" First, there is a serious assumption here that we are more merciful than God when in fact God is infinitely merciful. Further, God is happy in heaven, yet He knows that not everyone will be there. Also, if we could not be happy in heaven knowing a loved one is not there, then we have placed our happiness in the hands of another. C.S. Lewis offers a profound insight into this situation in a scene he wrote in *The Great Divorce:*

> "What some people say on earth is that the final loss of the soul gives the lie to all the joy of those who are saved."
> "Ye see it does not."
> "I feel in a way that it ought to."
> "That sounds very merciful: but see what lurks behind it."
> "What?"
> "The demand of the loveless and the self-imprisoned that they should be allowed to blackmail the universe: that till they consent to be happy (on their own terms) no one else shall taste joy: that theirs should be the final power; that Hell should be able to *veto* Heaven."

For example, a hungry person's refusal to take the gift of food to relieve his painful hunger should not veto the happiness of the generous person to enjoy his dinner.

Also, we can help our nonbelieving friends understand that their decision now could be the key to their current family members coming to Christ before they die and have no further chance to consider Christ (Hebrews 9:27). Furthermore, their decision could profoundly affect the lives of future generations of family members. It is also helpful to give any examples we know about of those who may have at one time felt torn between Christ and their current family, and who eventually decided to choose Christ.

Reflection

1. When we encounter barriers in our witness to others we should ask ourselves, Is their primary barrier first and foremost a barrier to correctly *understanding* Christianity or is it a barrier to their *embracing* Christianity? Remember, how you answer this question will dictate what your next step should be in your witness to them.

2. Remember that in today's world, to provide people palatable and plausible answers about our Christian faith, we may need to use an illustration or story first to help them accept the general principle we're trying to communicate. Then and only then can we make the inference to the theological implications of that agreed upon understanding.

3. Have you ever noticed how often people's objections to God and His standard of righteousness seem to be based on their own personal standard? In doing so, are they not placing God on trial based on what they think He should be like? To make spiritual progress with such people, we must help them reexamine some of these assumptions before what we say will strike a chord with them. Only then might we be able to make spiritual progress in our conversations with them.

4. A correct understanding about the God we worship and a correct understanding about who we are in relationship to Him is foundational to correctly answering many of the questions and challenges we may hear about God and the Bible.

Application

1. Listen carefully to the objections a person raises against God to detect erroneous, presupposed ideas of who He is. Explore these premises with the objector to help him see these judgments about God for himself. Clearing up wrong ideas on the very nature of God will provide valuable insights for the person struggling to understand God and the Bible.

2. Explore for yourself those passages of Scripture that speak about the transcendent and unapproachable holiness of God (e.g., Isaiah 6:1-7; Habakkuk 1:13; Hebrews 12:28-29). Use this knowledge to see anew the wonderful news of reconciliation, which is through Christ alone.

Chapter 9

Countering Common Misconceptions that Affect Evangelism

David: Do you think it matters what we have faith in, or is the important thing simply that we have faith?

Student: I think there are several different kinds of faith. I think you can have faith in love, faith in religion, faith in God, faith in your family. I think faith in general is very important. You've got to trust something, and fate or your faith or whatever, I think it's vital.

David: Would you agree that it is not faith per se but the object of our faith that's important for Christians, because Paul said in 1 Corinthians 15, "If Christ has not been raised, your faith is futile"?

Student: I don't know what to say to that…I like the idea of having a faith in general, since I have so many objects of my faith. I don't want to say that it's important to reach those goals, or whatever you're looking for. But I just say that faith in general is pretty important.

David: Do you have faith in elevators?

Student: Yeah, I'll ride anything.

David: But don't you look and check to make sure there's a floor there before you step into an elevator?

Student: No…I just go.

David: But don't you think it's a good idea to check to make sure there's a floor there before you step into the elevator?

Student: Essentially that would be a good idea.

David: So it's important not only that we have faith, but that we have faith in the right object.

Student: Yes, I would agree with that.

We cannot deny that our fruitfulness in evangelism has been affected by the kind of world we live in today. Yet many of us may be unaware that this crisis in how the world thinks has had a devastating influence on the thinking of the average Christian as well. In his book *Love Your God with All Your Mind,* Christian apologist J.P. Moreland asks the sobering question, "How is it possible for a person to be an active member of an evangelical church for twenty or thirty years and still *know next to nothing* about the history and theology of the Christian religion, the methods and tools required for serious Bible study, and the skills and information necessary to preach and defend Christianity in a post-Christian, neopagan culture?"[1]

The problem has arisen in part because of some common misconceptions Christians have that affect their understanding of their faith. But some of these misconceptions also affect our appreciation and use of pre-evangelism in our witness to others. Three of the most common are:

1. What do we mean by biblical faith (faith must have an object)?

2. What part does reason play in someone coming to Christ (belief *that*/belief *in* distinction)?

3. What does it mean in 1 Peter 3:15 to be ready to give an answer?

We will explain each of these issues, showing how a correct understanding can aid us in our witness to others.

What Is Biblical Faith?

Some people see biblical faith as believing something that cannot be demonstrated as true so it must be accepted blindly. But biblical faith includes not just the faith of the believer but also the object of our faith. Many Christians today don't understand this simple truth. Pollster George Barna says, "About one out of four (26%) born again Christians believe that it doesn't matter what faith you follow because they all teach the same lessons."[2] Yet, the apostle Paul said in 1 Corinthians 15:14, "And if Christ has not been raised, our preaching is useless and so is your faith."

So our faith is only as valid as the object in which it is placed. What is important is not faith itself, but rather the object of our faith. Paul warns us to be careful about what we put our faith and trust in. Just because we are sincere in our beliefs about something doesn't mean there is any merit to our belief. A lot of foolish things are taught as true that no one should believe. We would be wise not to act upon a belief if there is no evidence to support it.

Most of us would never trust a doctor to perform open heart surgery on us without first finding some evidence that he or she is a competent doctor. In a similar way, we should check out a religious truth claim before we embrace it as true and commit our lives to it.

What gives faith its merit is the object of that faith. And what gives faith its credibility is the evidence we have for the trustworthiness of that object. Once we clearly understand the biblical perspective on faith, we will see the greater need for engaging others in pre-evangelistic dialogue because the content of our faith is what's important, not mere belief in "something."

The Relation of Faith and Reason

But not only do Christians have a misconception about what biblical faith is, they also have a misconception about the relationship between faith and reason. More specifically, what part does reason play in someone coming to Christ? Not understanding how to answer this question plays a large role in why many Christians are unprepared to respond to the influences of skepticism, relativism, pluralism, and postmodernism.

Scripture helps us to understand the proper relationship between faith and reason. First, the Bible does not imply in any way that biblical faith is a "blind" faith. As we have demonstrated elsewhere, Jesus Himself used reason and evidence in calling on people to believe. The Old and New Testament writers provide us with substantial evidence to support the claim that God exists and that He has revealed Himself in the person of Jesus Christ. One of the important things that separates Christianity from other major religions is that Christianity stands or falls on one single event in history, the resurrection of Jesus Christ. If the resurrection did not occur, then Christianity is worthless. If it did (and the evidence is great that it did),[3] then Christianity is true.

Furthermore, biblical faith is not a blind faith but a reasonable faith. The following brief sampling from Scripture provides evidence to support this truth.

- God's blessings and provision for Israel. The blessing given to Israel reinforces God's case for exclusive worship of Him alone. Israel was God's apologetic to convince the nations to turn their hearts toward Him and also to bring about God's sovereign plan for saving all mankind (Genesis 12:3; Psalm 67:7).

- the miracles performed by God's prophets Moses (Exodus 7:5) and Elijah (1 Kings 18:20-38)

- the miracles performed by Jesus and His apostles (John 20:30-31; Acts 5:12-16; 2 Corinthians 12:12; Hebrews 2:1-4)

Furthermore, we are commanded to love God with our mind. In Mark 12:29-30 Jesus quotes the Old Testament and says, "Hear, O Israel! The Lord our God is one Lord; and you shall love the Lord your God with all your heart, and with all your soul, and with all your mind, and with all your strength" (NASB). Biblical faith then is a faith supported by evidence (John 21:25; 1 John 1:1-2).

But some may say, "I thought Christianity was a leap of faith?" Not so. It is neither a "leap" nor a "leap in the dark." It is a step of faith in the light—the light of sufficient evidence.

Consider the following illustration. A person wants to ascend to the top of a building. He pushes the button and two elevator doors open. The interior of the first is so totally dark that you cannot even see the floor clearly, and no one gets off it. The second is well lit, and a large man emerges from it. Which is the safer elevator? Which one provides you with the best evidence that it can get you to the top floor safely? True, it still takes a step of faith to get into the second one. But it is a step of faith in the light of good evidence. The other is a leap of faith in the dark. Christianity is like the second elevator.

Even when evidence—even good evidence—is present, faith is needed. But I can trust God for what I don't know because of what He has revealed to me that I do know. Biblical faith involves trusting God in areas that I do not have sufficient knowledge but do have adequate evidence that the one I am trusting is trustworthy.

This might seem unwise to some. But many of our everyday decisions involve faith in people, principles, or things that we do not have full knowledge of. We cannot cross a street, drive a car, sit in a chair, or turn on a light switch without some degree of faith or trust.

In the same way, biblical faith involves trusting God in areas that we may have some but not full understanding. We can know from reason alone that God exists (Romans 1:20), but we could never know from reason alone that this God exists eternally in three persons. A Christian can trust God in areas he does not fully comprehend because he has good reason to believe that God is trustworthy based on what we know about Him.

Further, biblical faith is a step of faith because it goes beyond reason but not against it. God has revealed things to us in His Word that go beyond our ability to fully understand or comprehend by reason alone, but they never go against reason. For example, the Christian doctrine of the Trinity is a mystery but not a contradiction. God is one nature with three persons, not three persons in one person or three natures in one nature, both of which are a contradiction.

Similarly, the doctrine of the incarnation does not mean that God became man by changing His nature from a divine to a human nature. Instead, the second person of the Trinity (His "whoness") took on a human nature (His "whatness") so that He has two *whats* (divinity and humanity), and yet remains one *who*.[4] Thus, Jesus was both God and man at the same time, but not in the same sense because His divine and human natures remained distinct—two different natures in one person. This is a mystery but not a contradiction.

So biblical faith includes evidence and reason, but it goes beyond reason although not against it. The Bible declares that God's thoughts are higher than ours (Isaiah 55:9), but God has revealed so much of who He is and has demonstrated His faithfulness in so many ways that we can trust Him in areas we do not fully comprehend. Biblical faith, then, can be defined as "trusting in what I have good reason to believe is true, even if the evidence is not exhaustive."

Someone may ask, "What part then does reason play in someone coming to faith in Christ?" To answer this question it's important to clarify the distinction between "belief *that*" and "belief *in*." For example, James points out that the demons "believe that" God exists (James 2:19), but we know that they do not "believe in" God. They have rational knowledge about God, yet they do not have a relational "belief in" God. In practical terms, this distinction means that when we witness to someone, we always point out two decisions that need to be made about Christ. First, one has to decide if there is sufficient evidence to "believe that" Jesus really is who He claimed to be. Once this has been accepted, then comes the more difficult decision: whether to put one's faith and trust in Christ by "believing in" Him. One could have good reasons for believing that Jesus really is God, but still not believe in Him.

Let's return to the elevator illustration. A thoughtful person has good evidence *that* the elevator can get him where he wants to go before he takes the step of faith and believes *in* the elevator. Likewise, a reasonable person should have sufficient evidence *that* God exists and *that* Christ is the Son of God who died for his sins and rose again before he places his faith *in* Christ. Belief *in* without prior evidence that it is true is blind faith.

We often hear people say, "Just trust in Jesus." But a reasonable person asks, "Which Jesus?" The Jesus of liberalism did not rise from the dead. The Jesus of Jehovah's Witnesses is a created being, Michael the Archangel. And the Jesus of Mormonism is a spirit being who is the spirit brother of Lucifer. None of these Jesus figures can save. One's faith is no better than its object. Only faith in the historic Jesus of Nazareth, the eternal Son of God, who died for our sins and rose again from the dead can save (Romans 10:9; 1 Corinthians 15:1-8).

Apologetics bears on the question of "belief that" but not "belief in." For example, someone may have good reasons to believe, based on the evidence, that another person would make a great spouse, but that doesn't force him or her to say "I do" to that person. That is a decision of the will, not merely the intellect.

Therefore, the evidence for Christianity can never force one to believe in Christ, despite how strong the evidence is. Evidence bears on the question of "belief that" but not "belief in." Faith in Christ means trusting in Christ's death on the cross as sufficient payment for sins and living one's life in accordance with this truth. Biblical faith involves more than just an intellectual agreement that Jesus is the Messiah; it also includes a daily commitment to and trust in the God of the universe who revealed Himself in the person of Christ (John 1:12). True biblical faith will also result in God's transforming power in our lives to change us from the inside out (Romans 12:2; Philippians 2:13).

This distinction has major implications for how we do evangelism. Apologetics cannot argue someone into the kingdom. Scripture teaches that the Holy Spirit *must* work in a person's life if he or she is to accept Christ. Jesus said in John 6:65, "No one can come to me unless the Father has enabled him." Therefore, faith and reason must work hand in hand to effectively reach others for Christ. Apologetics can help someone to "believe that" Jesus is the Messiah, but it can never force one to "believe in" Him.

Nonetheless, apologetics can play an important role for several reasons:

- Apologetics can help clear intellectual obstacles to faith, giving free course for the Holy Spirit to convict of sin and convert the sinner.

- Apologetics can help convince the Christian that his faith is reasonable.

- Apologetics can provide a higher degree of certainty of the truth of Christianity so as to make the Christian more willing and ready to do evangelism.

Paul "spoke so effectively that a great number of Jews and Gentiles believed" (Acts 14:1). Later he reasoned with the pagans at Lystra that God did not leave Himself "without testimony" (Acts 14:17), providing them with evidence from general revelation so they are "without excuse" (cf. Romans 1:19-20). Also, Paul regularly went to the synagogue and "reasoned with them from the Scriptures, explaining and proving that the Christ had to suffer and rise from the dead" (Acts 17:2). As a result, "some of the Jews were persuaded and joined Paul and Silas, as did a large number of God-fearing Greeks and not a few prominent women" (17:4). Later on Mars Hill, he reasoned with the philosophers, citing evidence in nature (17:26-29), and as a result, "a few men became followers of Paul and believed. Among them was Dionysius, a member of the Areopagus, also a woman named Damaris, and a number of others" (17:34).

Clearly, God used apologetics to help bring people to faith in Christ, and it can and should play an important role in our evangelism today. Its effectiveness, however, depends on our sensitivity in understanding how it can and cannot be used. But we can conclude that there is no real conflict between faith and reason.[5]

Being Ready to Give an Answer

First Peter 3:15 tells us to be ready to give an answer whenever someone asks us for the reason we believe what we do. We may never run across someone who asks tough questions about our faith, yet we should still be ready to respond if someone does.

In a post-Christian and anti-Christian culture, it is more and more likely that most Christians will be called on to answer tough questions. One of the indications of this is the success of the book coauthored with Ravi Zacharias, *Who Made God? And Answers to Over 100 Other Tough*

Questions of Faith. It was almost throwaway material from another book, but it has outsold its mother volume because people have been asked tough questions and need answers.

Some people have the mistaken notion that this means we only respond to questions asked by the nonbeliever. "Being ready," however, means more than just waiting for someone to ask us a question. The word for "being ready" in the Greek (*hetoimos*) is the same word used to refer to our anticipating ("being ready for") Christ's return (Matthew 24:44; Luke 12:40). So in 1 Peter 3:15, "being ready" means to anticipate nonbelievers' questions or objections.

If we combine 1 Peter 3:15 with 2 Corinthians 10:5 and 1 Corinthians 9:22, it is clear that our responsibility as Christians is to *eagerly anticipate* the questions and objections our non-Christian friends may raise. "Being ready is not just a matter of having the right information available, it is also an attitude of readiness and eagerness to share the truth of what we believe."⁶ Furthermore, we must be ready to give adequate answers to troubling questions, *whether we are asked a specific question or not.* This was the apostle Paul's practice in Acts 17 in speaking to the polytheists. He did not wait for them to raise objections or concerns; he took the offensive and pointed out the discrepancies in their beliefs (Acts 17:23-29).

Similarly, we are to anticipate the questions and spiritual concerns of nonbelievers just as a mother may eagerly anticipate the needs of her children and have cold glasses of juice waiting for them when they're done playing outside in the heat. This is the mind-set we need to develop in our witness to others. We have a responsibility to remove the obstacles and help people take steps toward Christ whether they ask us a specific question or not.

This clarification about what it means to "be ready" has major implications. If it truly is our responsibility to help our nonbelieving friends take one step closer to Jesus every day, as 1 Corinthians 3:6 and 1 Corinthians 9:22 imply, and if it is legitimate to practice the apologetic task by removing any potential barriers to faith in Christ, whether expressed or not, then this will cause a radical shift in how we do evangelism. In every encounter with our friends, we will try to discern what are the major obstacles keeping them from trusting Christ. In every conversation we will look for opportunities to build bridges by ask thought-provoking questions that potentially could move our conversation in a spiritual direction. Each moment we speak with our nonbelieving friends we will try to anticipate and remove obstacles they may encounter in their journey to the cross. All of this will be seen not as something supplemental, but as something fundamental to our responsibility to be a disciple of Jesus Christ in the world.

If 1 Peter 3:15 implies that one of the ways we make Christ Lord in our life ("sanctify Christ as Lord" NASB) is by giving an answer, and if it is clear that giving an answer means not only giving answers to stated concerns but also anticipating obstacles that may affect someone's spiritual journey, then how can we truly make Christ Lord in our lives if we are not looking for opportunities each day to help our nonbelieving friends take one step closer to Jesus?

May God help us to understand, like the men of Issachar, the times in which we live (1 Chronicles 12:32) and therefore know what we should do.

Reflection

1. Do you agree with the authors that clarifying the three key misconceptions Christians have about their faith might lead them to see a greater need and desire to use apologetics in evangelism?

2. Remember that if it is legitimate to use apologetics to remove any of our nonbelieving friends' barriers to faith in Christ, whether expressed or not, this will cause a radical shift in how we do evangelism. In every encounter we have with our friends, we will try to discern the obstacles keeping them from trusting Christ and look for opportunities to build bridges by asking thought-provoking questions that could move them a step closer.

3. We may acknowledge that the Bible commands us in 1 Peter 3:15 to give an answer to the questions people ask us about our Christian faith. Many of us attempt to obey

the letter of the law for this command, but what would it mean practically if we also were to obey the spirit of this command?

4. If it is really true that what gives our faith its merit is the object of our faith, and what gives our faith its credibility is the evidence we have for the trustworthiness of that object, then what can and should we change in our witnessing to reflect that belief?

Application

1. Do you agree with the authors that some of the misconceptions Christians have about their faith have affected our appreciation and use of pre-evangelism in our witness to others? If so, what can you do in your church to help clarify some of these misconceptions in the minds of other Christians?

2. Now that I have a clearer understanding of the proper role of faith and reason in my witness to others, I will (fill in the blank) _____
_____from this day forward.

3. In light of what you learned about what it means in 1 Peter 3:15 to "be ready to give an answer," what can you do practically to make Christ more and more Lord of your life as it relates to your apologetics and evangelistic task?

4. Pray that the Lord will grant you a heart of compassion for those in your circle of influence who do not yet know Christ. Pray also that the Holy Spirit would be your source of strength and wisdom. Now, go into all the world in meekness and in the knowledge of the truth, sharing with others by your life and words the Savior you've come to know, and helping them take one step closer to Him each day.

Conclusion

If we are going to see more people come to Christ, we need to truly understand the times we live in. In today's world this means that pre-evangelism needs to be an essential part of our evangelistic training and focus. By adopting some of the principles enumerated in this book, we believe it's possible to see evangelism not only as an obligation, but as something we actually enjoy doing and that makes a difference in the lives of our friends, family members, coworkers, and acquaintances.

Yet it is possible that some of you may feel a little overwhelmed by all the steps and procedures outlined in this book. You may even feel unsure whether you can actually do most or even some of the things we've suggested. Perhaps it would be helpful then to review some of the things we talked about in the Introduction to ensure we are not disheartened by this process.

First, we need to remember that the art of engaging others in spiritual dialogue takes time and practice, especially in a culture that is increasingly unsympathetic to the Christian perspective. We also need to remember that we must learn to crawl in our witness to others before we can walk, and we have to learn how to walk before we can run with confidence. Or to change the illustration, just as we may have skinned our knees a few times before we mastered riding our first bicycle, so too in learning this model we may face a few "accidents" along the way. But just as we didn't let a few bruises and scrapes deter us from our goal of riding a bike, neither should we be deterred from learning new skills that could lead to greater fruit, regardless of the minor obstacles we encounter along the way.

To be effective in pre-evangelism we need to remember to first focus on the fundamentals. First, we need to redefine what we commonly mean by evangelism, remembering that evangelism is a process (1 Corinthians 3:6). Every day we can help our nonbelieving friends take one step closer to Jesus Christ by what we say and how we live. Second, sometimes it is more effective to allow others to surface the truth for themselves through the use of thought-provoking and probing questions (2 Timothy 4:3-4).

Also, to ensure that our pre-evangelistic approach is holistic, we need to see the process as consisting of at least *four different kinds of conversations* with our nonbelieving friends: Hearing Conversations, Illuminating Conversations, Uncovering Conversations, and Building Conversations. Each of these corresponds to a specific role we should play in those friends' lives: that of *musician, artist, archaeologist,* and *builder.* We need to remember also that while we always want to start with Hearing Conversations, where we direct our focus next depends on where that person is and the leading of the Holy Spirit. As such, practicing pre-evangelism is more of an art than a science.

Furthermore, in order to maximize our effectiveness we need to keep in mind the three Ds of asking questions. Our goal should be to ask questions that surface their *doubt* (uncertainty) in their beliefs, while minimizing *defensiveness,* and yet creating a *desire* (curiosity) to hear more.

We also need to answer their questions in a way that will help build bridges to the cross. So by remembering to look for the real issue or question behind each question that is raised, we might be able to play a part in helping someone take one step closer to Christ.

While these steps may be helpful in increasing the effectiveness of our witness, we should never forget that our methods are of only secondary importance. For *our problems in evangelism are primarily not ones of methodology but of maturity.* Do we have a heart for God and do we care about the things God cares about the most (lost people)? If we have God's heart, then we will do whatever legitimate thing we can to advance

God's kingdom and His purposes in every conversation we have with our nonbelieving friends. What is most important then is that you and I develop a greater heart and passion for God and a greater concern for the lost around us.

Why don't we have a greater heart for reaching the lost? When I (David) was in college, I used to sit on a bench next to the student center and watch people walk by. On one occasion I started to cry because I realized in a greater way at that moment the sobering truth that if no one told these people about Christ, they would be separated from God for all eternity. Yet I don't seem to have the same kind of compassion for the lost and passion for God that I used to. I think there are at least three reasons why this may be so. Maybe you can identify with some of these struggles.

First, for some of us it may be that *we are not totally convinced of the truth of Christianity* (John 8:32). I once had a conversation with a college student who said he was a Christian but admitted he was not actively sharing his faith with others. I asked why, to which he replied, "I believe that Jesus is the way, the truth, and the life, but I don't believe it strongly enough that I'm willing to tell others."

Unfortunately, many Christians are beginning to question the very bedrock of their faith. A recent poll by Pew Forum on Religion and Public Life revealed that 57 percent of evangelical church attenders in the U.S. said they believe many religions can lead to eternal life.[1] This should not be surprising since we live in an age when so many are questioning the biblical story of Jesus. We saw this happen a few years ago with the popularity of *The Da Vinci Code* book and movie. Next we saw this with the acceptance by some of the alternative story about Jesus in *The Lost Gospel of Judas*. We saw the traditional Christian story further challenged with the hypothesis of *The Lost Tomb of Jesus*. And Philip Pullman's popular His Dark Materials trilogy (*The Golden Compass, The Subtle Knife,* and *The Amber Spyglass*) is "a direct attack on Christianity, the church, and God Himself."[2]

As a result, not only are many nonbelievers questioning the traditional understanding of Christianity, but even some Christians are surfacing doubts about their faith, in spite of any solid evidence to the contrary. I told the college student who had doubts, "If you have questions, find the answers you're looking for. As Christians we don't need to be afraid of the truth." Jesus Himself instructed His disciples, "You will know the truth, and the truth will make you free" (John 8:32 NASB). The apostle Paul reminds us that the fact of Christ's resurrection is central to our faith; if the resurrection did not happen, our Christianity is worthless (1 Corinthians 15:12-20). Luke in his Gospel similarly reminds us that these things were written "so that you may know the certainty of the things you have been taught" (Luke 1:4).

Therefore, as Christians we need to find the answers to those troubling questions that keep us from moving forward in our service and devotion to God. For when we are convinced that Jesus is who He claims to be, and we see His power manifested in our lives and the lives of our friends in a greater way, we will be more compelled to share that Good News with people in our circle of influence. If we truly understand what Jesus can do, we too, like Peter and John, will not be able to stop speaking of what we have experienced about Christ (see Acts 4:20). We need to heed the admonition of Elijah the prophet to quit wavering between two opinions and commit our lives to the One who is worthy of our total allegiance and worship (1 Kings 18:21).

So to increase a greater heart for God and have a greater compassion for the lost, we first *need to be convinced of the truth of the Christian message we proclaim.*

Second, *we don't realize the extent to which we have been forgiven* (Luke 7:47). This may have come about because we have forgotten who we are apart from Christ. How many of us are convinced that the sins we have committed are worthy of *eternal punishment and separation from God?* Unfortunately, we forget as Christians that the Bible teaches that all of us fall short of God's standard (Romans 3:23) and that all of our righteousness is to God "like filthy rags" (Isaiah 64:6).

Even as Christians, we may not always be honest with ourselves as well as with God about our spiritual condition apart from Christ. How many of us are convinced that apart from God's miraculous grace in our lives we could commit the kinds of crimes that Hitler did? Until we have this understanding, we won't begin to understand our human depravity and the depth of our sin. And until we understand the depth of our sin, we won't fully appreciate the depth of God's forgiveness given to us when we trusted Christ.

In Luke 7 Jesus was dining with Simon, a Pharisee, and spoke to him about the sinful woman who was wetting His feet with her tears, wiping them with her hair, and pouring perfume on them. Jesus told the indignant Pharisee, "I tell you, her many sins have been forgiven—for she loved much. But he who has been forgiven little loves little" (v. 47).

If we fail to remember how much we were forgiven, it will affect our passion and heart for serving the Lord. When you and I realize how much God loves us by understanding how much He has forgiven us, it will free us up to serve Him, not out of duty or obligation but out of love. We will care about the things God cares about, and we will have the capacity to love others because of the love we experienced from God. For Scripture itself teaches us, "We love because he first loved us" (1 John 4:19).

We will then serve God in the long haul because we are serving Him with the right motive, not out of a sense of duty or obligation, but as an overflow of our gratitude for what He has done for us. To the degree that we have understood how much we have been forgiven, to that degree we will understand how much God loves us.

Third, *we forget the urgency of the task.* Let's be honest—many of us feel so beaten down by life's trials that we consider it a victory just to make it through the day. It's easy for us to develop tunnel vision and focus only on our immediate, temporal, and material concerns and miss the bigger picture and a more eternal perspective. We forget how urgent it is for us to share the Good News with others.

Jesus reminds us in a hyperbolic statement that "if your right hand makes you stumble, cut it off and throw it from you; for it is better for you to lose one of the parts of your body, than for your whole body to go into hell" (Matthew 5:30 NASB). As serious a consequence as it is to lose an arm or leg, it is even more serious to be separated from God for all eternity. Therefore, the most loving thing we can ever do is to tell others the Good News that has the power to transform lives today and guarantee a future and a hope tomorrow.

Why do we struggle with having a great heart for God and passion for the lost? It may be that *we are not convinced of the truth of Christianity.* It also might be because *we don't realize the extent of our forgiveness.* Finally, it may also be because *we forget the urgency of the task.* Once these barriers are overcome and God creates in us a greater heart for Him and a passion for reaching the lost, then the tools provided in this book for doing pre-evangelism may create more open doors for the Gospel.

May God help all of us to be more creative in how we witness to others today so that more and more people can hear and respond to the Gospel message. May we also learn how to do it in such a way that we too are more eager to look for ways to share that Good News today, tomorrow, and for the rest of our lives!

Evangelism and Apologetics Resource List

Books and Articles

Level 1

You're just starting out! You need the basics of the Christian faith at a level you can comprehend. You may also have a non-Christian friend who would benefit from resources that are easier to understand. Those marked with an asterisk (*) are great for non-Christians too.

Doctrine:	*The Essentials of the Faith,* 14 DVDs, Norman Geisler, www.InternationalLegacy.org
	* *Know What You Believe,* Paul Little
	* *Basic Christianity,* John Stott
Relational Evangelism:	*Becoming a Contagious Christian,* Bill Hybels
	Larry Moyer's How-To Book on Personal Evangelism, Larry Moyer
	Out of the Saltshaker and into the World, Rebecca Pippert
Apologetics:	*Living Loud,* Norman Geisler and Joseph Holden
Who Is Jesus?:	* *More Than a Carpenter,* Josh McDowell
	* *Is Jesus God?* John Maisel (located at www.meeknessandtruth.org)
	* *Jesus: God, Ghost, or Guru?,* Jon Buell
Common Questions:	* *Know Why You Believe,* Paul Little

Level 2

You've been at it for a while. You need to go a bit deeper because you've been sharing your faith regularly and you're often running into deeper questions.

Doctrine:	*Conviction Without Compromise*, Norman Geisler and Ron Rhodes
	A Survey of Bible Doctrine, Charles Ryrie
	Charts of Christian Theology and Doctrine, Wayne House
Relational Evangelism:	*Living Proof*, Jim Petersen
	Evangelism Made Slightly Less Difficult, Nick Pollard
	Finding Common Ground, Tim Downs
	True for You, But Not for Me, Paul Copan
Apologetics:	*New Evidence That Demands a Verdict*, Josh McDowell
	I Don't Have Enough Faith to Be an Atheist, Norman Geisler and Frank Turek
	When Skeptics Ask, Norman Geisler
Who Is Jesus?:	* *A Case for Christ*, Lee Strobel
	* *Jesus Among Other Gods*, Ravi Zacharias
	The Cross of Chirst, John Stott
Common Questions:	*Who Made God? And Answers to Over 100 Other Tough Questions of Faith*, Ravi Zacharias and Norman Geisler
	I'm Glad You Asked, Kenneth Boa and Larry Moody
	* *Mere Christianity*, C.S. Lewis
	* *A Case for Faith*, Lee Strobel

Faith and Reason: *Love Your God with All Your Mind,* J.P. Moreland

Dealing with Hard Passages: *The Big Book of Bible Difficulties,* Norman Geisler and Thomas Howe

Hard Sayings of the Bible, Peter Davids, F.F. Bruce, Manfred Brauch, and Walter Kaiser

Dealing with Worldviews: *The Universe Next Door,* James Sire

Dealing with Darwinism: *Defeating Darwinism by Opening Minds,* Philip Johnson

Darwin on Trial, Philip Johnson

A Politically Incorrect Guide to Darwinism, Jonathan Wells

The Design of Life, William Dembski and Jonathan Wells

Evolution: The Fossils Still Say No!, Duane Gish

Dealing with Mormons: *Reasoning from the Scriptures with Mormons,* Ron Rhodes

Speaking the Truth in Love to Mormons, Mark Cares

Dealing with Watchtower: *Reasoning from the Scriptures with the Jehovah's Witnesses,* Ron Rhodes

Jehovah's Witnesses Answered Verse by Verse, David Reed

Dealing with New Age: *The Infiltration of the New Age,* Norman Geisler and J. Yutaka Amano

Dealing with Islam: *Reaching Muslims for Christ,* William Saal

Dealing with Atheism: *A Shattered Visage: The Real Face of Atheism,* Ravi Zacharias

Can Man Live Without God?, Ravi Zacharias

Level 3

You're beginning to give your life to reaching the lost and constantly find yourself in tough witnessing situations.

Doctrine:
Systematic Theology (4 vols), Norman Geisler

Major Bible Themes, Lewis Sperry Chafer

Relational Evangelism:
Telling the Truth: Evangelizing Postmoderns, D.A. Carson

Who Is Jesus?:
* *The Case for the Resurrection of Jesus,* Gary Habermas and Michael Licona

The Resurrection of Jesus, Gary Habermas

Apologetics:
Why I Am a Christian, Norman Geisler and Paul Hoffman

Twelve Points That Show Christianity Is True, 12 DVD lectures, Norman Geisler, www.InternationalLegacy.org

Reasonable Faith, William Lane Craig

Handbook of Christian Apologetics, Peter Kreeft and Ronald Tacelli

Affirming Intelligent Design:
The Design Revolution, William Dembski

Answering Postmodernism:
The Gagging of God, D.A. Carson

Dealing with Relativism:
Relativism, Francis Beckwith and Gregory Koukl

The Abolition of Man, C.S. Lewis

Truth in Religion, Mortimer Adler

Common Questions:
When Critics Ask, Norman Geisler and Thomas Howe

When Skeptics Ask, Norman Geisler and Ronald Brooks

Dealing with Cults:	*Kingdom of the Cults,* Walter Martin
	The Changing World of Mormonism, Sandra Tanner
	Countering the Cults, Norman Geisler and Ron Rhodes
Dealing with Chinese Beliefs:	*A Biblical Approach to Chinese Traditions and Beliefs,* Daniel Tong
	Faith of Our Fathers, Chan Kei Thong
Dealing with Islam:	*Answering Islam: The Crescent in Light of the Cross,* Norman Geisler and Abdul Saleeb
Dealing with New Age:	*Apologetics in the New Age,* Norman Geisler and David Clark
Dealing with Reincarnation:	*The Reincarnation Sensation,* Norman Geisler and J. Yutaka Amano
Dealing with Worldviews:	*Worlds Apart: A Handbook on World Views,* Norman Geisler and William Watkins
World Religions:	*The Compact Guide to World Religions,* Dean Halverson
	Neighboring Faiths, Winfried Corduan

Level 4

Apologetics:	*Christian Apologetics,* Norman Geisler
	Baker Encyclopedia of Apologetics, Norman Geisler

Helpful Apologetic Websites

- Access Research Network: www.arn.org
- Apologetics Index: www.apologeticsindex.org
- Bible Query: www.biblequery.org
- Christian Answers Network: www.christiananswers.net
- Christian Research Institute (Hank Hanegraaff): www.equip.org
- William Lane Craig: www.leaderu.com/offices/billcraig
- The Evangelism Toolbox: www.evangelismtoolbox.com
- Norman Geisler: www.normgeisler.com
- Leadership University: www.leaderu.com
- Meekness and Truth (David Geisler): www.meeknessandtruth.org
- Probe Ministries (Kerby Anderson): www.probe.org
- Reasons to Believe (Hugh Ross): www.reason.org
- Stand to Reason (Greg Koukl): www.str.org
- Watchman Fellowship, Inc. (for help with cults): www.watchman.org
- Ravi Zacharias International Ministries: www.rzim.org
- For working with Muslims: www.answering-islam.org; www.gnfcw.com
- For working with Hindus: www.karma2grace.org/

Appendix 1

PRE-EVANGELISM CONVERSATION STRATEGIES

Developing a Strategy for Reaching Our Friends, Family Members, Coworkers, and Acquaintances

Person's name			
Step 1 (Hear) **HEAR** the *sour notes* people are singing	*What am I hearing?*	*What am I hearing?*	*What am I hearing?*
Ask Yourself • What do they believe? • What worldview framework do they hold? • What does their heart long for that Jesus can provide?	*Type of "sour note"*	*Type of "sour note"*	*Type of "sour note"*
• What are the sour notes (discrepancies or inconsistencies) that I hear in their viewpoint?	*Example 1*	*Example 1*	*Example 1*

Types of Inconsistencies	*Example 2*	*Example 2*	*Example 2*
• belief vs. heart longing			
• they believe one thing but their heart longs for something else			
• belief vs. behavior	*Example 3*	*Example 3*	*Example 3*
• they believe one thing but the way they live or behave is different from what they say they believe			
• belief vs. belief			
• they hold two or more beliefs that contradict each other in some way	*Example #___*	*Example #___*	*Example #___*
• illogical belief			
• their belief is contradictory and unmeaningful merely in making the statement			
What one "sour note" should I focus on in my conversation with them?			

Step 2 (Illuminate) HELP people surface the truth for themselves	*Ask yourself:*	*Ask yourself:*	*Ask yourself:*
• that uncover the meaning of unclear terms • that sur-face their uncertainties	*What terms might I need to clarify?*	*What terms might I need to clarify?*	*What terms might I need to clarify?*
Determine the *impact* of your question by asking whether it: • surfaces doubt (uncertainty) • minimizes defensiveness • creates desire (curiosity) to hear more	*How exactly should I phrase my question?* *One follow-up question:* *One thought-provoking question to create inter-est for further dialogue*	*How exactly should I phrase my question?* *One follow-up question:* *One thought-provoking question to create inter-est for further dialogue*	*How exactly should I phrase my question?* *One follow-up question:* *One thought-provoking question to create inter-est for further dialogue*

Step 3	Ask yourself:	Ask yourself:	Ask yourself:
UNCOVER their real barriers to the Gospel (i.e., dig up their history and find out how they came to be where they are in their beliefs) • determine if legitimate • determine nature of barrier • uncover emotional gbaggage • uncover questions or issues • discover biggest barrier • uncover motivational factors • uncover volitional factors	*Major Obstacle* *Examples of uncovering questions:*	*Major Obstacle* *Examples of uncovering questions:*	*Major Obstacle* *Examples of uncovering questions:*

Step 4	Ask yourself:	Ask yourself:	Ask yourself:
BUILD a positive case for Christ and look for opportunities to invite them to trust Him			
(consider what may be the most important information you gleaned from steps 1-3 to help you build a strategy of moving from pre-evangelism to evangelism)	*How do I build common ground? (Where do my friends and my interest intersect?)*	*How do I build common ground? (Where do my friends and my interest intersect?)*	*How do I build common ground? (Where do my friends and my interest intersect?)*
• find a balance			
• common ground	*What planks do I use to construct my bridge?*	*What planks do I use to construct my bridge?*	*What planks do I use to construct my bridge?*
• bridge building			
• memorize an outline			
• remember the goal			
• transition to evangelism	*What kind of bridges (heart or head) will be most effective in witnessing to my friend?*	*What kind of bridges (heart or head) will be most effective in witnessing to my friend?*	*What kind of bridges (heart or head) will be most effective in witnessing to my friend?*

	Strategy for Building Bridges:	*Strategy for Building Bridges:*	*Strategy for Building Bridges:*

GOSPEL PRESENTATION

Colossians 4:2-4

PRAY for yourself	**PRAY for the opportunity**	**PRAY for your coworkers**
Pray for God to give you the wisdom and strength to be a good witnesses in how you speak God's truth to those around you.	*Pray for open doors to plant seeds of the Gospel with others.*	*Pray for your boss, clients, customers, friends, colleagues, family members— asking God to move in their lives.*

Appendix 2

PRE-EVANGELISM CONVERSATION TRAINING

Step 1

- **Listen carefully** to determine where they are coming from
- **Hear** the *sour notes* people are "singing" to us
- **Seek for clarification...**

Ask yourself:

- What do they believe?
- What worldview framework do they hold?
- What do their hearts long for that Jesus can provide?
- What are the sour notes that I hear?
- What are the inconsistencies in their belief systems?

Ask them:

- I think I understand. What you are saying is... Is this right?

Types of inconsistencies:

- belief vs. heart longing
  - they believe one thing but their hearts long for something else
- belief vs. behavior
  - they believe one thing but the way they live or behave is different from what they believe
- belief vs. belief
  - they hold to two or more beliefs that contradict each other in some way

- illogical belief
  - their particular belief is contradictory and unmeaningful merely in making the statement

Examples:

A Buddhist believes in achieving a state of nirvana that can only be achieved by letting go of their identity. Yet in reality people would not want to let go of their identity because to do so would mean losing all conscious awareness of who they are.

A Muslim believes that his good deeds must outweigh his bad deeds to get to heaven. Yet some may not pray even five times a day.

An atheist/freethinker believes that God does not exist. Yet they have difficulty living their life without believing in nonmaterial things such as truth, love, and beauty.

An extreme postmodernist believes there are absolutely no absolutes (there is no meta-story).

Step 2

- **Help** people *surface* the truth for themselves

Ask them questions:

- that uncover the meaning of unclear terms
- that surface their uncertainties
- that expose false beliefs

Determine the *impact* of your question by asking whether it *(the 3 Ds of asking questions)*:

- surfaces *doubt* (uncertainty)
- while it minimizes *defensiveness*
- yet creates a *desire* (curiosity) to hear more

Remember to focus on those *stand-out* inconsistencies rather than pointing out all inconsistencies.

Further amplification:

- What do you mean when you say...?
- How is it possible...?
- Ask yourself, what is one key question that could surface some doubt about their current beliefs?
- Ask yourself, am I asking the question in a way that will make it difficult for them to get defensive right away?
- Ask yourself, am I ending the spiritual dialogue in a way that they might be willing to continue the conversation later or even hear more what I'm saying about Jesus?
- Ask yourself, what is one key thing I can focus on that could unlock openness for further dialogue?

Examples:

What do you mean when you say you are an _____ (atheist, freethinker, agnostic)?

How is it possible for all religions to be the same when some of them contradict each other'?

How can Jesus be merely a man when He lived a sinless life, fulfilled prophecy, and gave evidence for His resurrection from the dead?

I am curious, why do you need Jesus to save you if you can measure up?

How do you fit Jesus into your religious beliefs?

I am curious, how do you fit in your thinking both _____ and _____?

Do you know what Jesus taught about the issue of desire that Buddha was so concerned about?

Can you think of any natural way to explain the fact of the empty tomb and yet believe that Jesus was just a man, as many claimed?

Step 3

- **Uncover** their *real barriers* to the Gospel (i.e., dig up their history and find out how they came to be on their current path)

Ask yourself:

- What is the barrier/obstacle?
    - Is the issue a real concern or is it a smoke screen?
    - Is the barrier intellectual or emotional, or both?
    - What is the specific emotional baggage they are carrying?
    - Is there a question or issue behind the question raised?
    - What is their biggest barrier to the Christian faith?
    - What would motivate them to get answers?
    - Is there a volitional barrier?

To surface their history and baggage:

- ask questions that surface false beliefs or distortions about concepts/theological principles
- use illustrations

Two types of obstacles:

- **Obstacles in their *understanding* of Christianity**
    - thinking there is no difference in religious beliefs (pluralism)
    - not understanding the nature of sin
    - not understanding that salvation is by grace and not by works
    - reconciling the problem of evil with the existence of God

- **Obstacles in their *embracing* of Christianity**
  - their sinful and selfish nature (Jeremiah 17:9)
  - being overly concerned with making a living and acquiring material possessions
  - feeling negative toward Christians because they think that they have the only way to God
  - being indifferent toward anything of a religious nature
  - hypocrisy among Christians
  - believing that Christianity is a Western concept and should have no place in an Eastern culture

Examples of uncovering questions:

- So what you are saying is...
- If you could know the truth about religious issues, would you want to know it?
- If I could answer your question in a way that would make sense to you, would that help you to more seriously consider a belief in God and Christianity?
- Out of all the questions you have about Christianity, what is that one question that is right now keeping you from embracing Christianity?
- What do you consider the biggest obstacle in your religious tradition (Buddhist, Hinduism, Islam) that would keep you from embracing Christianity?

Step 4

- **Build** a *positive* case for Christ and look for *opportunities* to invite them to trust Him

Ask yourself:

- What is the right balance in your approach (objective evidence vs. subjective experience)?

- Where can you find common ground in your discussion (i.e., where your beliefs and theirs intersect)?
- What is your strategy for building a bridge that uses planks of common understanding that also takes into account when to build head or heart bridges?
- What do you need to keep in mind in building your bridge and yet not lose sight of the goal?
- What types of conversations would lead to open doors to transition to share the Gospel?

Further amplification:

Do they need to see evidence of Christ's power manifested first in how I live my life, or do they need to understand how miraculous Jesus' life is and how unique He is compared to other religious leaders?

We are to find that point of intersection between our beliefs and theirs.

These planks can be built on common understanding, even those things they are not aware of.

Has anyone ever explained to you the difference between *do* versus *done?*

Examples of bridge-building questions:

- Example of a *heart bridge*

If you had a choice between having a relationship with a God who created you and wanted you to see Him as your loving Father, or a relationship with an impersonal God or one who you could never be sure of His love and concern for you, which one would appeal to you?

- Example of a *head bridge*

Did you know that Buddha claimed to point to the way, and Muhammad claimed to be a prophet of God, but Jesus Christ is the only major religious leader who claimed to be God, who lived a sinless life, fulfilled prophecy, and then died on the cross and rose from the dead?

• Example of a *head bridge*

If you were coming to the end of your life, and you met Jesus and other great religious leaders and each one suggested a different path, whose advice would you take? Wouldn't you take the advice of someone who's been to the other side and came back to tell us about it?

GOSPEL PRESENTATION

HEARING THE INCONSISTENCIES IN PEOPLE'S BELIEFS

Identify which of the following four "sour notes" or inconsistencies occurs in the examples of people's beliefs listed below.

1. Belief vs. Heart Longing

2. Belief vs. Behavior

3. Belief vs. Belief

4. Illogical Belief

Example 1

A. I believe there isn't anything that's absolutely right or wrong.

B. I believe it's important to treat others with respect and civility.

Which sour note is this? _____

Example 2

A. I believe that as long as my material needs are met, that is all that really matters.

B. All of us hunger for truth, love, knowledge, justice, and significance.

Which sour note is this? _____

Example 3

A. God is so far from us that we cannot know anything about Him.

Which sour note is this? _____

Example 4

A. I believe my good deeds must outweigh my bad deeds to get to heaven.

B. I don't really pray five times a day.

Which sour note is this? _____

Example 5

A. I believe that reality is just something that man constructed and does not exist nor is it real.

B. All of us desire to live a life that is real and that has meaning and purpose.

Which sour note is this? _____

Example 6

A. I am a Christian.

B. I am not sure why Jesus had to die on the cross.

Which sour note is this? _____

Example 7

A. I believe that the Bible is reliable.

B. I believe that Jesus is just one of the many ways to God.

Which sour note is this? _____

Example 8

A. I cannot speak a word of English.

Which sour note is this? _____

Example 9

A. I don't believe in an afterlife, whether it is heaven or hell.

B. I believe that all the terrorists will be punished for killing innocent people.

Which sour note is this? _____

Example 10

A. I believe the Bible is reliable.

B. I believe I must do good works to be saved.

Which sour note is this? _____

Example 11

A. I don't think that religion is really necessary.

B. Sometimes I pray, but I don't feel I'm getting any response.

Which sour note is this? _____

Example 12

A. Always avoid making absolute statements.

Which sour note is this? _____

Example 13

A. I am absolutely sure that you should not come to any conclusions about what is right or wrong.

Which sour note is this? _____

Example 14

A. Buddhists believe in achieving a state of nirvana that can be achieved only by letting go of their identity.

B. In reality Buddhists would not want to let go of their identity because to do so would mean losing all conscious awareness of who they are.

Which sour note is this? _____

Example 15

A. You should always be tolerant of people of different religious beliefs, except those who are not tolerant.

Which sour note is this? _____

Example 16

A. Muslims believe that Allah is so far removed from us that even the spiritual leaders (Imams) who try to get close to him are not able.

B. A Muslim desires to know God in a deeper and more personal way.

Which sour note is this? _____

Example 17

A. I believe that Jesus is just a great prophet.

B. I believe that Muhammad supersedes previous prophets, including Jesus, being the last and greatest prophet, summing up God's final revelation to mankind. Yet the Qur'an teaches that Jesus was born of a virgin and lived a life without sin, but Muhammad was born of natural birth and did sin.

Which sour note is this? _____

Example 18

A. I don't believe there is such a thing as right and wrong.

B. I try to live a good life.

Which sour note is this? _____

Example 19

A. You should be skeptical about everything.

Which sour note is this? _____

Example 20

A. I am an atheist.

B. I go to the Buddhist temple sometimes to pray for success in my career.

Which sour note is this? _____

Example 21

A. As a Buddhist I believe we must not desire anything.

B. I buy lottery tickets at least once a month.

Which sour note is this? _____

Example 22

A. I believe my nature is basically good.

B. I don't like it when my colleague is promoted ahead of me.

Which sour note is this? _____

Example 23

A. There isn't any absolute right or wrong.

B. The Japanese military leaders during World War II were wrong to have killed millions of Chinese and Asians.

Which sour note is this? _____

Example 24

A. Many Hindus believe in an impersonal god.

B. There is a hunger in Hindus to know God in a deeper and more personal way.

Which sour note is this? _____

Example 25

A. I believe that all human beings are reincarnated after death. If they are bad, they will become an animal.

B. I believe that the human population in this world is getting bigger and that there is an increase in crime.

Which sour note is this? _____

Answers:
Example 1: Belief vs. Belief
Example 2: Belief vs. Heart Longing
Example 3: Illogical Belief
Example 4: Belief vs. Behavior
Example 5: Belief vs. Heart Longing
Example 6: Belief vs. Belief
Example 7: Belief vs. Belief
Example 8: Illogical Belief
Example 9: Belief vs. Belief and Belief vs. Heart Longing
Example 10: Belief vs. Belief
Example 11: Belief vs. Behavior
Example 12: Illogical Belief
Example 13: Illogical Belief
Example 14: Belief vs. Heart Longing
Example 15: Illogical Belief
Example 16: Belief vs. Heart Longing
Example 17: Belief vs. Belief
Example 18: Belief vs. Behavior (or Belief vs. Heart Longing)
Example 19: Illogical Belief
Example 20: Belief vs. Behavior
Example 21: Belief vs. Behavior
Example 22: Belief vs. Behavior
Example 23: Belief vs. Belief
Example 24: Belief vs. Heart Longing
Example 25: Belief vs. Belief

Appendix 4

MORE ALLEGED SOUR NOTES AMONG CHRISTIAN BELIEFS

The Alleged Sour Note of Biblical Contradictions

Space does not permit examination of all the alleged contradictions in the Bible. *The Big Book of Bible Difficulties: Clear and Concise Answers from Genesis to Revelation* (Norman L. Geisler and Thomas Howe) lists some 800 alleged contradictions, none of which turn out to be real ones. The book gives reasons why the Bible cannot err (because it is God's Word and God can't err) and also the most common mistakes critics make in assuming the Bible errs. Augustine's dictum applies well to this situation: "If we are perplexed by any apparent contradiction in Scripture, it is not allowable to say, The author of this book is mistaken; but either [1] the manuscript is faulty, or [2] the translation is wrong, or [3] you have not understood" (Augustine, *Reply to Faustus 11.5*).

The truth is that the critics have made the errors, not the Bible. A few examples will suffice:

Cain married when there were no women to marry. God created Adam and Eve, and they had two sons, Cain and Abel. After Cain killed Abel (Genesis 4:8), he found a wife and married her (4:17). Critics question where Cain's wife came from, with the implication that the biblical account of the creation of the human race must be wrong. But we are not told how much time elapsed between the murder of Abel and Cain's finding a wife. Adam had other "sons and daughters" over a period of 800 years (5:3-5), so there were more than enough girls available for Cain to marry.

Life can't exist without light. But the Bible speaks of life on the third day (Genesis 1:13), and the sun was not made until the fourth day (1:14-15), which, according to science, was millions of years later. However, since it is possible that most scientists may be wrong about the long age of the earth, the critic errs because Genesis affirms that there was light on the first day (1:3). It was only later that the sun became distinctly visible in the sky (perhaps as the vapor evaporated).

The inscription on Jesus' cross reads four different ways in the four Gospels. The critics claim that all four accounts can't be true. However, the critics wrongly assume that a partial report is a false report. But this is not necessarily so. Each Gospel gives part of the inscription—the crucial part—namely, the one who claimed to be "the king of the Jews" was being crucified. No Gospel said it was anyone else but Jesus, and all the Gospels said He claimed to be "the king of the Jews."

Matthew 28:5 says there was one angel at the tomb, but John (20:12) says there were *two* angels there. Again, this is not a contradiction, because wherever there are *two,* there is always *one.* It never fails! Matthew did not say *only* one angel was there. The critic has to add a word to make it contradictory.

Matthew 27:5 says Judas "hanged himself," yet Acts 1:18 declares "he fell headlong, his body burst open and all his intestines spilled out." This difficulty is easily resolved by the following likely scenario: Sometime after Judas hanged himself, his body was discovered and the rope was cut (since it was contrary to the law to touch a dead body). The body fell on rocks and it burst open.

Joshua 10:12 says "the sun stood still," but modern science informs us that the sun does not move around the earth. Joshua also speaks of the sun rising (1:15), but this is not thought to be contradictory. Even contemporary meteorologists speak of "sunrise" and "sunset." No scientist says, "Honey, look at the beautiful earth rotation!" The truth is that the Bible, like modern scientists, speaks in everyday observational language. And from an observer's point of view, the sun rises and moves across the sky and sets.

First Kings 11:1 approves of polygamy, yet elsewhere the Bible supports monogamy (1 Corinthians 7:2; 1 Timothy 3:2). But here the critic errs by assuming that the Bible approves of everything it records. The Bible records Satan's lie (Genesis 3:4; cf. John 8:44) but does not approve of lying (Exodus 20:16). Likewise, it records David's adultery (2 Samuel 11), but does not approve of it (Exodus 20:14).

First Kings 4:26 says Solomon had 40,000 stalls for his chariot horses. Yet 2 Chronicles 9:25 says there were only 4,000. But there is no evidence that the number 40,000 was in the original text that God inspired (2 Timothy 3:16). This kind of copyist error (adding an extra zero) is easy to make. But they are rare and affect no doctrine of Scripture. Certainly no critic would not pick up his money if he heard from the lottery: "Y#U HAVE WON TEN MILLION DOLLARS." In spite of the minor error, 100 percent of the message comes through.

In brief, no one has ever demonstrated an irreconcilable error in the inspired text of Scripture. The errors are in the critics of the Bible, not in the Bible itself.

The Alleged Sour Note of Ethical Contradictions

Most atheists argue that the God of the Bible cannot be all-powerful and all-perfect and yet permit the evil that is in this world. Their argument can be put in logical form like this:

1. If God is all-powerful, He could defeat evil.
2. If He is all-good, He would defeat evil.
3. But evil is not defeated.
4. Therefore, there is no such God.

The problem with this argument is obvious. Premise 3 is incomplete. It should read: Evil is not *yet* defeated. But given this revised premise, the conclusion in Premise 4 does not follow. Simply because He has not yet defeated evil doesn't mean He never will.

Indeed, the argument from evil does not disprove God. Rather, it proves God. For as former atheist C.S. Lewis put it, we cannot claim there is no God because there is evil and injustice in the world. For we cannot know that something is unjust unless we know what is just. And if we know there is a moral law of justice, then there must be a Moral Lawgiver (God). So, rather than disprove God, the presence of evil proves God.

The Alleged Sour Note Within Certain Christian Beliefs

The Doctrine of the Trinity. That there are three distinct persons in one and only one being (essence) seems flatly contradictory to many unbelievers. Muslims believe it is a form of polytheism—with three gods. But this is not what orthodox Christians believe. For they affirm that there is only one God, but there is a plurality of persons within this one Deity.

Others believe it is a violation of the law of noncontradiction. How can God be three and only one at the same time? The answer is that He can because He is one and three *in a different sense.* He is one in His nature but three in His persons.

Many Muslims believe the eternal Qur'an is one with God and yet distinct from Him. Likewise, one's mind, ideas, and words expressing them are one, and yet they are distinct. God is love, and love involves a lover, a loved one, and a spirit of love between them; even so, God is three in one. Or to change the analogy, God is three *whos* in one *what.* There is a Father *who,* a Son *who,* and a Holy Spirit *who,* but only one divine nature (*what*).

Believing that God is three persons in one nature is certainly a mystery, though it is not a real contradiction. It would be a contradiction if we were to confess that God is three natures in one nature or three essences in one essence. So while God is one and many at the same time, He is not one and many in the same sense. He is one in the sense of His essence but many in the sense of His persons. (See Norman L. Geisler, *Baker Encyclopedia of Christian Apologetics* [Grand Rapids, MI: Baker Books, 1999], 732, for further clarification of the doctrine of the Trinity.)

Appendix 5

KEY QUESTIONS TO ASK NON-CHRISTIANS

Questions for Atheists

1. Are you absolutely sure there is no God? If not, then is it not possible that there is a God? And if it is possible that God exists, then can you think of any reason that would keep you from wanting to look at the evidence?

2. Would you agree that intelligently designed things call for an intelligent designer of them? If so, then would you agree that evidence for intelligent design in the universe would be evidence for a designer of the universe?

3. Would you agree that *nothing* cannot produce *something*? If so, then if the universe did not exist but then came to exist, wouldn't this be evidence of a cause beyond the universe?

4. Would you agree with me that just because we cannot see something with our eyes—such as our mind, gravity, magnetism, the wind—that does not mean it doesn't exist?

5. Would you also agree that just because we cannot see God with our eyes does not necessarily mean He doesn't exist?

6. In the light of the big bang evidence for the origin of the universe, is it more reasonable to believe that no one created something out of nothing or someone created something out of nothing?

7. Would you agree that something presently exists? If something presently exists, and something cannot come from nothing, then would you also agree that something must have always existed?

8. If it takes an intelligent being to produce an encyclopedia, then would it not also take an intelligent being to produce the equivalent of 1000 sets of an encyclopedia full of information in the first one-celled animal? (Even atheists such as Richard Dawkins admit this volume of information exists in the first one-celled animal.)[1]

9. If an effect cannot be greater than its cause (since you can't give what you do not have to give), then does it not make more sense that mind produced matter than that matter produced mind, as atheists say?

10. Is there anything wrong anywhere? If so, how can we know unless there is a moral law?

11. If every law needs a lawgiver, does it not make sense to say a moral law needs a Moral Lawgiver?

12. Would you agree that if it took intelligence to make a model universe in a science lab, then it took super-intelligence to make the real universe?

13. Would you agree that it takes a cause to make a small glass ball found in the woods? And would you agree that making the ball larger does not eliminate the need for a cause? If so, then doesn't the biggest ball of all (the whole universe) need a cause?

14. If there is a cause beyond the whole finite (limited) universe, would not this cause have to be beyond the finite, namely, not-finite or infinite?

15. In the light of the anthropic principle (that the universe was fine-tuned for the emergence of life from its very inception), wouldn't it make sense to say there was an intelligent being who preplanned human life?

Questions for an Agnostic

1. Of the two possible kinds of agnostic, which kind are you: 1) Strong agnostic who says we can't know anything for

sure? or 2) Weak agnostic who says we don't know anything for sure (but we could if we had enough evidence)?

2. If you are the strong kind, then how do you know for sure that you can't know anything for sure?

3. If you are the weak kind of agnostic, then is it not possible that we could know for sure that God exists (if we had enough evidence)?

4. Do you agree that an open-minded person should be willing to look at all the evidence? If so, then are you willing to look at the evidence for God's existence?

Questions for a Muslim

1. Do you pray five times a day? If you have not done the minimum requirement for a Muslim, how can you be sure you are going to get to heaven?

2. How can Jesus be considered a great prophet when the Gospels say many times that Jesus accepted worship as God (Matthew 8:2; 14:33; 28:9; Luke 24:52; John 9:38; 20:28-29)?

3. If our Bible today is corrupted, then how do we know what parts are corrupted?

4. How can the Bible be corrupted when Muhammad told people to read it (Sura 5:68; 10:94) and we have manuscripts showing that the Bible of Muhammad's day was substantially the same as the one we have today?

5. How can you believe the Qur'an when it states that "none can change His word" (Sura 6:115; see also 6:34; 10:64), yet it also says that the Bible is God's previous revelation (Sura 2:136; 4:163)? Yet you believe that Jesus never claimed to be God but merely claimed to be a prophet, and somehow the Bible got corrupted because it teaches that Jesus claimed to be God.

6. If killing is wrong for religious reasons, then why does the

Qur'an prescribe the killing of unbelievers (Sura 9:5,29; 47:4)?

7. How can heaven be described as a place full of wine and women when this is the kind of life Allah forbids here (Sura 78:32)?

8. Why do Muslims believe Muhammad is superior to Jesus when even the Qur'an affirms that Jesus was sinless (Sura 3:45-46; 19:19-21), born of a virgin (Sura 3:47), called the Messiah (Sura 3:45), performed miracles such as raising the dead (Sura 5:110), and bodily ascended into heaven (Sura 4:158), and Muhammad did none of these things?

9. If many Muslims believe that the Qur'an is the eternal Word of God and yet different from God, then why can't Jesus be the eternal Son of God and yet different from God?

10. If Allah can do whatever He pleases, then why could He not allow His prophet Jesus to die on the cross and raise Him to life again?

Questions for a Hindu

1. Can you explain why some Hindus believe there is one reality beyond good and evil, and yet they live as though they believe evil is real?

2. If reincarnation is a result of deeds in a previous life, then how did the first reincarnation begin?

3. If those suffering in this life are being punished for deeds in a previous life, then why show any compassion to help the downtrodden and needy? Are we not just tinkering with their karma and delaying their punishment to a further life?

4. If evil is not real, then how did the illusion begin? Why is it so universal? And why does it seem so real?

5. If we must undergo a changing process of enlightenment to discover we are one with the Absolute, then how can we

be the Absolute since it is unchanging and never underwent such a process?

Questions for a Buddhist

It is important in speaking with a Buddhist that you ask questions instead of assuming you know what they believe. Beliefs of individual Buddhists often differ from Buddha's teachings. Furthermore, there are many folk beliefs, such as praying to Buddha for help in the struggles of daily life, that contain a mixture of different beliefs. Below are some clarifying questions, existential questions, and follow-up questions you should consider asking:

Clarifying Questions to Ask a Buddhist:

1. Why have you personally adopted Buddhistic beliefs?
2. What does Buddhism teach about who we are?
3. What do you believe happens to us after we die?
4. What hope does Buddhism offer you personally?

Existential Questions for a Buddhist:

1. What does Buddhist teaching do for you personally?
2. What problems does this teaching solve?
3. What hope does Buddhism offer you personally?

Follow-up Questions for a Buddhist:

1. Is there any way to know whether we should choose one religion over another?
2. How can you determine if Buddhism is true?
3. If Buddhism teaches that desire is wrong, how does your practice of Buddhism fit with your desire to win the lottery?
4. Doesn't the law of karma only postpone the solution to

the problem of evil and suffering, but never really solves the problem?

5. If the death of Christ satisfied the punitive demands of the righteous laws of God, then what need would there be for more payment (see Romans 3:25-26; Hebrews 2:17; 1 John 2:2; 4:17-18)?

6. If there is no continuity with your self after death, then how can it be the same person who is being rewarded in the next life?

7. If it is not the same person who is reborn into another body, then why should someone pay for the karmic debt left by someone else?

8. Is it not true that if there is an ultimate moral law, then there is an ultimate Moral Lawgiver?

9. And if there is no ultimate moral law, then why should we follow the Buddhist 10 Precepts and the Eight-fold "Right" paths and reincarnation based on actions?

10. Is it true that Buddhism teaches that we are in reality an aspect of God and in some respects less than real as an individual? If so, how did this metaphysical amnesia arise and come to pervade and dominate our whole experience?

11. How can we know that the world of our senses is an illusion (not real) unless we know a backdrop of reality against which we can make this judgment?

12. Does not the goal to eliminate all desire involve the desire to eliminate all desire?

13. If we should eliminate all desire, how about the desire to have children, help others, enjoy life, and experience nirvana?

14. Would it not be better to redirect desire to God who alone can fulfill than to eliminate all desire (Matthew 4:4; 5:6; 6:33)?

Questions for Those in Taoist/Buddhist Folk Religions

1. Who sets the standard for goodness? Would it ever be possible for you to reach that standard?

2. What will you be in the next life? Are you confident that you will make it there?

3. Who can assure you of that final destination and destiny?

4. Do you think there is a way to be certain what the heavens want so that we can please them?

5. Do you think offering food to your dead ancestors once a year will be enough?

6. Do you know how long you will have to do this until your ancestor is reborn?

7. When will you know when you can stop offering the paper money?

8. Should there not be a way to keep one's descendants, who are still on earth, informed so as not to waste their time and money? Otherwise, the paper money will be pocketed by someone not related to you, and you will not even know about it.

9. Would you like to hear about the One and Only God, Shang Ti, whom even the great Chinese emperors worshipped?

Bibliography

Books

Aldrich, Joseph C. *Life-Style Evangelism: Crossing Traditional Boundaries to Reach the Unbelieving World*. Portland, OR: Multnomah Press, 1981.

Baker, David Reed. *Jehovah's Witnesses Answered Verse by Verse*. Grand Rapids, MI: Baker Books, 1986.

Barna, George. *Evangelism That Works: How to Reach Changing Generations with the Unchanging Gospel*. Ventura, CA: Regal Books, 1995.

Carson, D.A., ed. *Telling the Truth: Evangelizing Postmoderns*. Grand Rapids, MI: Zondervan, 2000.

Chan, Edmund. *Growing Deep in God*. Singapore: Covenant Evangelical Free Church, 2002.

Chopra, Deepak. *The Seven Spiritual Laws of Success*. San Rafael, CA: Amber-Allen Publishing and New World Library, 2007.

Clark, David K. *Dialogical Apologetics: A Person-Centered Approach to Christian Defense*. Grand Rapids, MI: Baker Books, 1993.

Collins, Francis. *The Language of God: A Scientist Presents Evidence for Belief*. New York: Free Press, 2007.

Colson, Charles, and Nancy Pearcey. *How Now Shall We Live?* Wheaton, IL: Tyndale House Publishers, 1999.

Copan, Paul. *"True for You, But Not for Me": Deflating the Slogans that Leave Christians Speechless*. Minneapolis: Bethany House Publishers, 1998.

Dawkins, Richard. *The God Delusion*. Great Britain: Transworld Publishers, 2006.

Dembski, William. *The Design Revolution: Answering the Toughest Questions About Intelligent Design*. Downers Grove, IL: InterVarsity Press, 2004.

Downs, Tim. *Finding Common Ground: How to Communicate with Those Outside the Christian Community…While We Still Can*. Chicago: Moody Publishers, 1999.

Geisler, Norman L. *Baker Encyclopedia of Christian Apologetics*. Grand Rapids, MI: Baker Books, 1999.

_____. *Christian Apologetics*. Grand Rapids, MI: Baker Books, 1976.

_____. *Creation in the Courts*. Wheaton, IL: Crossway, 2007.

_____. *False Gods of Our Time*. Eugene, OR: Harvest House Publishers, 1985.

_____. *Knowing the Truth About Creation: How It Happened and What It Means for Us*. Ann Arbor, MI: Servant Books, 1989.

_____. *Miracles and the Modern Mind: A Defense of Biblical Miracles*. Grand Rapids, MI: Baker Books, 1992.

_____. *Systematic Theology*. Vol. 4. Minneapolis: Bethany House Publishers, 2005.

_____, and Kerby Anderson. *Origin Science: A Proposal for the Creation-Evolution Controversy*. Grand Rapids, MI: Baker Books, 1987.

_____, and Peter Bochino. *Unshakable Foundations*. Minneapolis: Bethany House Publishers, 2001.

_____, and William E. Nix. *A General Introduction to the Bible*. Chicago: Moody Publishers, 1986.

_____, and Frank Turek. *I Don't Have Enough Faith to Be an Atheist*. Wheaton, IL: Crossway, 2004.

_____, and William D. Watkins. *Worlds Apart: A Handbook on World Views*. 2d ed. Eugene, OR: Wipf and Stock Publishers, 2003.

Greeson, Kevin. *The Camel: How Muslims Are Coming to Faith in Christ*. Richmond, VA: WIGTake Resources, 2007.

Guinness, Os. *Fit Bodies, Fat Minds: Why Evangelicals Don't Think and What to Do About It*. Grand Rapids, MI: Baker Books, 1994.

Habermas, Gary R. *The Resurrection of Jesus*. Grand Rapids, MI: Baker Books, 1980.

Halverson, Dean, ed. *The Compact Guide to World Religions*. Minneapolis: Bethany House Publishers, 1996.

Hoyle, Fred. *The Intelligent Universe*. New York: Holt, Rinehart and Winston, 1983.

Hume, David. *A Letter from a Gentleman to His Friend in Edinburgh*. Edited by E.C. Mossner and J. V. Price. Edinburgh: University Press, 1967.

Hybels, Bill, and Mark Mittelberg. *Becoming a Contagious Christian*. Grand Rapids, MI: Zondervan, 1994.

Johnson, Phillip E. *Darwin on Trial*. Downers Grove, IL: InterVarsity Press, 1993.

Kaufmann, Walter. *Critique of Religion and Philosophy*. 3rd ed. Princeton, NJ: Princeton University Press, 1979.

Kumar, Steve. *Christianity for Skeptics: An Understandable Examination of Christian Belief*. Peabody, MA: Hendrickson Publishers, 2000.

Lewis, C.S. *Mere Christianity*. New York: Collier Books, 1952.

_____. *Miracles: A Preliminary Study*. New York: Macmillan Publishing Company, 1960.

Lipstadt, Deborah. *Denying the Holocaust: The Growing Assault on Truth and Memory*. New York: Free Press, 1993.

McCallum, Dennis, ed. *The Death of Truth*. Minneapolis: Bethany House Publishers, 1996.

McDowell, Josh. *The New Evidence That Demands a Verdict*. Nashville: Thomas Nelson Publishers, 1999.

Moreland, J.P. *Love Your God with All Your Mind: The Role of Reason in the Life of the Soul*. Colorado Springs: NavPress, 1997.

_____. *Scaling the Secular City: A Defense of Christianity*. Grand Rapids, MI: Baker Books, 1987.

Newman, Randy. *Questioning Evangelism: Engaging People's Hearts the Way Jesus Did*. Grand Rapids, MI: Kregel Publications, 2004.

O'Leary, Denyse. *By Design or by Chance? The Growing Controversy on the Origins of Life in the Universe*. Minneapolis: Augsburg Press, 2004.

Petersen, Jim. *Living Proof: Sharing the Gospel Naturally*. Colorado Springs: NavPress, 1989.

Pollard, Nick. *Evangelism Made Slightly Less Difficult*. Downers Grove, IL: InterVarsity Press, 1997.

Phillips, Timothy R., and Dennis L. Okholm, eds. *Christian Apologetics in the Postmodern World*. Downers Grove, IL: InterVarsity Press, 1995.

Poole, Garry. *Seeker Small Groups: Engaging Spiritual Seekers in Life-Changing Discussions*. Grand Rapids, MI: Zondervan, 2003.

Sire, James W. *The Universe Next Door: A Basic Worldview Catalog*. 3rd ed. Downers Grove, IL: InterVarsity Press, 1997.

_____. *Why Should Anyone Believe Anything at All?* Downers Grove, IL: InterVarsity Press, 1994.

Veith, Gene Edward, Jr. *Postmodern Times: A Christian Guide to Contemporary Thought and Culture*. Wheaton, IL: Crossway Books, 1994.

Zacharias, Ravi. *A Shattered Visage: The Real Face of Atheism*. Brentwood, TN: Woglemuth and Hyatt, Publishers, 1990.

_____. *Can Man Live Without God?* Dallas: Word Publishing, 1994.

_____, and Kevin Johnson. *Jesus Among Other Gods: The Absolute Truth of the Christian Message*. Nashville: Thomas Nelson Publishers, 2000.

Magazine Articles

Jastrow, Robert. An interview in *Christianity Today*, 6 August 1983, 15.

Web Articles

Barna, George. *Born Again Christians,* 2000, www.barna.org.

Bright, William. Quoted in *Jesus and the Intellectual,* www.billbright.com/intellectual/purpose.html (accessed 15 April 2006).

Craig, William Lane. "A Classic Debate on the Existence of God," November 1994 University of Colorado (Boulder) www.com/offices/billcraig/docs/craig-tooley0.html (accessed 2 February 2006).

Geisler, David N. "Problems and Pathways to the Gospel in a Postmodern World." Meekness and Truth Ministries. www.meeknessandtruth.org/tools.htm (accessed 19 March 2006).

Montoya, David. "Dealing with Both Minds and Hearts: Answering the Questions Behind the Questions." Meekness and Truth Ministries. www.meeknessandtruth.org/tools.htm (accessed 19 March 2006).

Unpublished Articles

Koons, Robert. "Effective Apologetics." Colorado Springs: International Students Incorporated Training, June 1998.

Notes

Chapter 1: The Need for Pre-Evangelism in a Postmodern World

1. Sheryl Crow, "Every Day Is a Winding Road," *Sheryl Crow* (Santa Monica, CA: A&M Records, 1996).

2. Gene Edward Veith, *Postmodern Times: A Christian Guide to Contemporary Thought and Culture* (Wheaton, IL: Crossway Books, 1994), 16.

3. J.P. Moreland, *Love Your God with All Your Mind* (Colorado Springs: NavPress, 1997), 21.

4. This is clearly seen in the writings of the Jewish historian Josephus. For example, a fourth-century Arabic text found in the tenth century probably reflects the original intent of Josephus, AJ, 18.3.3 who says, "he was perhaps the messiah concerning whom the prophets have recounted wonders" (cited in Josh McDowell, *The New Evidence That Demands a Verdict* [Nashville: Thomas Nelson, 1999], 57). This can also be seen in the admission in the Jewish Talmud that Jesus did do miracles, though they attributed this to the power of the devil. (See Sanhedrin 43a as cited in Josh McDowell, *The New Evidence*, 58.)

5. See Deborah Lipstadt, *Denying the Holocaust: The Growing Assault on Truth and Memory* (New York: Free Press, 1993).

6. Nick Pollard, *Evangelism Made Slightly Less Difficult* (Downers Grove, IL: InterVarsity Press, 1997), 31.

7. For a more detailed explanation of this point, see Paul Copan, *True for You, But Not for Me* (Minneapolis: Bethany House Publishers, 1998).

8. Ravi Zacharias and Kevin Johnson, *Jesus Among Other Gods* (Nashville: W. Publishing Group, 2000), 11.

9. By postmodern friends I mean those who do not think there is an overarching story (including Christianity) that can explain the big picture (See Jean-Francois Lyotard, *The Postmodern Condition: A Report on Knowledge* (Minneapolis: University of Minnesota Press, 1984), xxiv). They also tend to consider Christianity's exclusive beliefs at least offensive if not downright arrogant or intolerant.

10. See our website at www.meeknessandtruth.org to listen to our audio/PowerPoint presentation on conversational evangelism.

11. Although Jim Petersen suggested this approach almost 20 years ago in his book *Living Proof*, unfortunately this concept has not caught on until recently. See Jim Petersen, *Living Proof* (Colorado Springs: NavPress), 148.

12. Tim Downs, *Finding Common Ground: How to Communicate with Those Outside the Christian Community While We Still Can* (Chicago: Moody Press, 1999), 32.

13. I developed this definition in 2000 when I started Meekness and Truth Ministries.

14. I have learned much about this mirror concept of witnessing from Glenn McGorty, who originally pioneered an approach that we worked together on and in partnership with my home church, Hill Country Bible Church Northwest, Austin, TX. To learn more about the church model Glenn developed and the resources they have to train others, see the website: www.DIALOGRoadmap.org.

15. This issue is covered more fully in Norman L. Geisler and Patrick Zukeran, *The Apologetics of Jesus* (Grand Rapids, MI: Baker Books, 2009).

16. See the article "Problems and Pathways to the Gospel" at www.meeknessandtruth.org for the scriptural support for the integration of Christian evidences in our evangelism.

17. For example, Christian philosopher and theologian Philip D. Kenneson unapologetically says, "I don't believe in objective truth or relativism. Moreover, I don't want you to believe in objective truth or relativism either, because the first concept is corrupting the church and its witness to the world, while tilting at the second is wasting the precious time and energy of a lot of Christians" (Philip D. Kenneson, "There's No Such Thing as Objective Truth, and It's a Good Thing, Too" in Timothy R. Phillips and Dennis L. Okholm, eds. *Christian Apologetics in the Postmodern World* [Downers Grove, IL: InterVarsity Press, 1995], 156).

Chapter 2: Introduction to Conversational Evangelism

1. The late Francis Schaffer developed a similar approach in his witness to others, but he did not teach all the elements in the conversational model, and unfortunately he did not package it so that it could be reproduced and taught to others, as Dr. Bill Bright did with his transferable concept of the Four Spiritual Laws.

2. Brett Yohn (Baptist Student Ministry director, University of Nebraska) originally developed the imagery of artist, archaeologist, and engineer to describe the "Think model" process, which we now call Conversational Evangelism. To describe these four distinct roles of hearing, illuminating, uncovering, and building, we now use the imagery of musician, artist, archaeologist, and builder.

3. David Reed Baker, *Jehovah's Witnesses Answered Verse by Verse* (Grand Rapids, MI: Baker Books, 1986), 113.

4. Ibid.

5. See Nick Pollard, *Evangelism Made Slightly Less Difficult* (Downers Grove, IL: InterVarsity Press, 1997), 43, for a further explanation of positive deconstructionism.

6. See appendixes 1 and 2 for help mapping out a strategy with those you are trying to reach using this model.

7. According to Nick Pollard, "The process of positive deconstructionism recognizes and affirms the elements of truth to which individuals already hold, but it also helps them discover for themselves the inadequacies of the underlying worldviews they have

absorbed. The aim is to awaken a heart response that says, 'I am not so sure that what I believe is right after all. I want to find out more about Jesus'" (Pollard, *Evangelism Made Slightly Less Difficult*, 44).

8. I call this the boomerang principle because when people ask us questions, rather than answering their questions, we turn the question around on them so they feel the weight of it.

Chapter 3: Learning the Role of the Musician

1. *Contingent* means that it is, but it could not be. It exists, but it could go out of existence. Whatever is contingent, dependent, finite, and changing needs a cause for its existence. For a further discussion on this point of contingency and dependency, see Norman L. Geisler, "Cosmological Argument," in *Baker Encyclopedia of Christian Apologetics* (Grand Rapids, MI: Baker Books, 1999), 164-65.

2. Pascal said, "What else does this craving, and this helplessness, proclaim but that there was once in man a true happiness, of which all that now remains is the empty print and trace? This he tries in vain to fill with everything around him, seeking in things that are not there the help he cannot find in those that are, though none can help, since this infinite abyss can be filled only with an infinite and immutable object; in other words by God himself" (Pascal, *Pensees* #425).

3. Francis Collins, *The Language of God: A Scientist Presents Evidence for Belief* (New York: Free Press, 2007), 38.

4. Ravi Zacharias, *Jesus Among Other Gods* (Nashville: Thomas Nelson, 2000), 78.

5. Ibid., 71-72.

6. Robert Jastrow, *God and the Astronomers* (New York: W. W. Norton, 2000), 14, 115.

7. An interview in *Christianity Today*, 6 August 1983, 15.

8. Pliny the Younger (62?–c.113), in his correspondence in A.D. 106 with the emperor Trajan, reported that a genuine Christian would "bind themselves to a solemn oath, not to any wicked deeds, but never to commit any fraud, theft, adultery, never to falsify their word, not to deny a trust when they should be called upon to deliver it up."

Chapter 4: Learning the Role of the Artist

1. The person who taught me the importance of using this phrase in pre-evangelism was Glenn McGorty. Glenn was instrumental in developing a pre-evangelistic approach called "Mirror Model" at my home church, Hill Country Bible Northwest, Austin, TX. That model has evolved into the curriculum called "Dialog." To learn more about this approach go to www.DIALOGRoadmap.org.

2. Intelligent design proponent Phillip Johnson points out how elastic the word *evolution* can be. See Phillip Johnson, *Darwin on Trial* (Downers Grove, IL: InterVarsity Press, 1991), 9.

3. William A. Dembski, *The Design Revolution* (Downers Grove, IL: InterVarsity Press, 2004), 271.

4. See Norman Geisler, *Creation and the Courts* (Wheaton, IL: Crossway Books, 2007), chapter 8.

5. For further examples see Norman L. Geisler and William E. Nix, *A General Introduction to the Bible* (Chicago: Moody Publishers, 1986), 408.

6. These are all actual things college students have communicated in surveys.

7. For more information, go to www.livingwaters.com.

8. Ray Comfort, who has taken thousands of people through the Ten Commandments, says, "Although millions know of the Ten Commandments, most can name only three or four, and very few actually understand the spiritual nature of the law." Personal e-mail from Ray Comfort on 28 December 2008.

9. Sura 5:48 says, "To thee (People of the Book) we sent the scripture in truth, confirming the scripture that came before it, and guarding it in safety: so judge between them by what Allah hath revealed, and follow not their vain desires, diverging from the truth that hath come to thee."

10. A.D. 117–138 John Rylands (fragment of John); A.D. 100–150 Chester Beatty Papyri; A.D. 125–175 Bodmer II (p66); A.D. 125–175 p104 (fragment of Matthew); 30 more manuscripts before A.D. 300; early church writers (from A.D. 97/98 to A.D. 200) referred to many verses in the Bible.

11. Matthew 8:2—leper; Matthew 28:9—women at the tomb; Matthew 14:33—the disciples; Matthew 28:17 and Luke 24:52—the disciples after Jesus rose; John 9:38—a blind man; John 20:28-29—Thomas called Him "my Lord and my God."

12. Deepak Chopra, *The Seven Spiritual Laws of Success* (Novato, CA: New World Library, 1994), 68-69.

13. Paul's argument in Acts 17:28-29 was that they had made these wooden gods, and yet in some sense they also believed these wooden gods had created them.

Chapter 5: Learning the Role of the Archaeologist

1. To learn more about the art of surfacing hidden barriers read David Montoya's unpublished article, "Dealing with Both Minds and Hearts: Answering the Questions Behind the Questions," located on the Meekness and Truth website (www.meeknessandtruth.org) under Evangelism Tools Library.

2. Edmund Chan, *Growing Deep with God* (Covenant, 2002), 48.

Chapter 6: Learning the Role of the Builder

1. Remember that in a positive deconstructive approach we are affirming the things we agree on even if we disagree on much more than we agree on. See Nick Pollard, *Evangelism Made Slightly Less Difficult* (Downers Grove, IL: InterVarsity Press, 1997), 44, for a more in-depth explanation of positive deconstruction.

2. Richard Dawkins, *The God Delusion* (New York: Houghton Mifflin, 2006), 73.

3. Ibid., 80. For example, one can state that there are absolutely no absolutes, just as

someone can say, "I cannot utter a word in English." Certainly both are sayable but both are not meaningful statements.

4. Unpublished paper from a former student giving an example of common ground.

5. See Fred Hoyle, *The Intelligent Universe* (New York: Holt, Rinehart and Winston, 1983), 176. Hoyle says, "Our results, together with further developments by William Fowler, Robert Wagoner and myself, became what even to this day is pretty well the strongest evidence for the big bang, particularly as the arguments were produced by members of what was seen as the steady state camp."

6. Most leading scientists now acknowledge that the Universe cannot be any older than 15 billion years. This is not enough time for the evolutionary process to form the complexity of life we observe today.

7. On numerous occasions when nonbelieving college students have been asked this series of questions, they surprisingly admitted that yes, some religious views must be wrong.

8. Ravi Zacharias, *Jesus Among Other Gods* (Nashville: Thomas Nelson Publishers, 2000), 12.

9. Christian researcher George Barna says "About one out of four (26%) born again Christians (in the West) believe that it doesn't matter what faith you follow because they all teach the same lessons."

10. The acrostic CAMEL corresponds to the following points taken from Sura 3:42-55—Chosen 3:42-44; Announcement 3:45-47; Miracle 3:48-49; Eternal Life 3:50-55.

11. Kevin Greeson, *The Camel: How Muslims Are Coming to Faith in Christ* (Richmond, VA: WIGTake Resources, 2007), 40. The Qur'an teaches that Isa is holy (Sura 3:42-48); Isa has power over death (Sura 3:49-54); Isa knows the way of heaven and is the way (Sura 3:55).

12. See Norman L. Geisler and Frank Turek, *I Don't Have Enough Faith to Be an Atheist* (Wheaton, IL: Crossway Books, 2004), chapters 1–15.

13. See N. Geisler, *Baker Encyclopedia of Christian Apologetics* for more details.

14. See Bill Hybels and Mark Mittelberg, *Becoming a Contagious Christian* (Grand Rapids, MI: Zondervan, 1994) for further documentation of *do* versus *done*.

Chapter 7: The Art of Asking Questions of People with Different Worldviews

1. Nick Pollard, *Evangelism Made Slightly Less Difficult* (Downers Grove, IL: InterVarsity Press, 1997), 71.

2. Norman L. Geisler and William D. Watkins, *Worlds Apart: A Handbook on World Views,* 2d ed. (Eugene, OR: Wipf and Stock Publishers, 2003), 11-12.

3. Pollard, *Evangelism Made Slightly Less Difficult,* 47.

4. Paul Copan, *"True for You, But Not True for Me"* (Minneapolis: Bethany House Publishers, 1998), 26.

5. Pollard, *Evangelism Made Slightly Less Difficult,* 35-36.

6. Ibid., 31-32.

7. Ibid., 41.

8. Ibid., 50.

9. Ibid., 77.

10. Geisler and Watkins, *Worlds Apart*, 266.

11. Norman L. Geisler, *Christian Apologetics* (Grand Rapids, MI: Baker Books, 1976), 233.

12. For a defense of this view see Geisler, *Christians Apologetics*, chapters 9–13.

13. See Geisler, *Christian Apologetics*, 143-44, for a clarification of the principle of undeniability.

14. A good example of this approach can be found in the writing of the late Christian apologist Francis Schaffer.

15. Francis Schaffer has a good illustration of this point cited in Norman L. Geisler, *False Gods of Our Time* (Eugene, OR: Harvest House Publishers, 1985), 85-86.

Chapter 8: The Art of Answering Objections While Moving Forward

1. See Nick Pollard, *Evangelism Made Slightly Less Difficult* (Downers Grove, IL: Inter-Varsity Press), 70.

2. This illustration was adapted from a wedding dress analogy used by Glenn McGorty in his Mirror Mode curriculum for evangelism training at Hill Country Bible Church Northwest, Austin, TX.

3. Ravi Zacharias, *Jesus Among Other Gods* (Nashville: Thomas Nelson Publishers, 2000), 9.

4. This concept was taken from Dean Halverson, ed., *The Compact Guide to World Religions* (Minneapolis: Bethany House Publishers, 1996), 62.

5. Romans 1:18-32 says that men have knowledge about God, but they turn away from Him. As a result, they have enough knowledge to condemn them, but not enough knowledge about God to save them.

6. Even the skeptic David Hume never claimed that something could arise without a cause. See David Hume, *A Letter from a Gentleman to His Friend in Edinburgh*, ed. E.C. Mossner and J.V. Price (Edinburgh: University Press, 1967).

7. See Norman L. Geisler, *Baker Encyclopedia of Christian Apologetics* (Grand Rapids, MI: Baker Books, 1999), 120-21, for a discussion of the principle of causality.

8. See Geisler, *Baker Encyclopedia of Christian Apologetics*, 291, for further clarification of this point.

9. C.S. Lewis, *Mere Christianity* (New York: Simon and Schuster Publishers, 1996), 45.

10. There is a difference between an *absence* and a *privation*. Blindness in a stone is an

absence of sight because a stone is not expected to see. However, blindness in a human being is a privation because sight is characteristic of a human being.

11. See Norman L. Geisler, *The Roots of Evil* (Eugene, OR: Wipf and Stock Publishers, 2002), for a discussion of all the major problems and solutions offered for the problem of evil.

12. See Geisler, *Baker Encyclopedia of Christian Apologetics*, 219, for a further explanation of this point.

13. William Lane Craig made this point in a debate with Michael Tooley. See "A Classic Debate on the Existence of God," November 1994, University of Colorado (Boulder), www.com/offices/billcraig/docs/craig-tooley0.html (accessed February 2, 2006).

14. See Norman L. Geisler, *Systematic Theology*, vol. 4 (Minneapolis: Bethany House Publishers, 2005), chapter 10.

15. Geisler, *Roots of Evil*, 59.

Chapter 9: Countering Common Misconceptions that Affect Evangelism

1. J.P. Moreland, *Love Your God with All Your Mind* (Colorado Springs: NavPress, 1997), 188.

2. George Barna, "Born Again Christians," 2000, www.barna.org.

3. See Gary R. Habermas, *The Resurrection of Jesus* (Grand Rapids, MI: Baker Books, 1980).

4. See Norman L. Geisler, *Baker Encyclopedia of Christian Apologetics* (Grand Rapids, MI: Baker Books, 1999), 732, for a discussion of this issue.

5. For a more comprehensive explanation of the role of faith and reason see Geisler, *Baker Encyclopedia of Christian Apologetics*, 239-43.

6. N. Geisler, *Baker Encyclopedia of Christian Apologetics*, 37.

Conclusion

1. Pew Forum on Religion and Public Life, http://pewforum.org/news/display.php?NewsID=15915.

2. Janie B. Cheaney, "Very Dark Material," *World*, 27 January 2001.

Appendix 5: Key Questions to Ask Non-Christians

1. Evolutionist Richard Dawkins acknowledges that "amoebas have as much information in their DNA as 1000 *Encyclopaedia Britannicas.*" Richard Dawkins, *The Blind Watchmaker* (New York: W.W. Norton and Co., 1996), 116.

Conviction Without Compromise

Standing Strong in the Core Beliefs of the Christian Faith

NORMAN GEISLER AND RON RHODES

❧

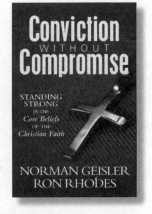

Ever wondered how to talk with believers who disagree with your beliefs without compromising sound doctrine? Norman Geisler, one of the nation's leading apologists, teams with Reasoning from the Scriptures president Ron Rhodes to explore the well-known saying, "In essentials, unity; in nonessentials, liberty; in all things, charity."

Beginning with essential doctrines such as the inspiration and inerrancy of Scripture, Christ's deity, and 14 others, *Conviction Without Compromise* provides solid scriptural defenses while showing how various movements have moved away from historic, biblical Christianity.

The authors show why Christians can disagree agreeably about more than a dozen important but nonessential beliefs, such as the nature of spiritual gifts, the role of women in the church, and the nature of sacraments.

Finally, the section on charity highlights some "rules of engagement" and explores lessons learned from church history.

A must-read for Christians who care about sharing their faith.